THE
LANGUAGE
OF
REAL
ESTATE
POCKET GUIDE

JOHN W. REILLY
MARIE S. SPODEK, DREI, CONTRIBUTING EDITOR

Dearborn™
Real Estate Education

This publication is designed to provide accurate and authoritative information in regard to the subject matter covered. It is sold with the understanding that the publisher is not engaged in rendering legal, accounting, or other professional service. If legal advice or other expert assistance is required, the services of a competent professional person should be sought.

President: Roy Lipner
Vice President of Product Development and Publishing: Evan Butterfield
Development Editor: Elizabeth Austin
Production Editor: Leah Strauss
Director of Production: Daniel Frey
Typesetter: Ellen Gurak
Creative Director: Lucy Jenkins

© 2006 by Dearborn Financial Publishing, Inc.®
Published by Dearborn™ Real Estate Education
30 South Wacker Drive, Ste. 2500
Chicago, IL 60606-7481
(312) 836-4400
http://www.dearbornRE.com

06 07 08 10 9 8 7 6 5 4 3 2 1

Library of Congress Cataloging-in-Publication Data
Reilly, John W.
  The language of real estate pocket guide / by John W. Reilly, Marie S. Spodek.
    p. cm.
  ISBN-13: 978-1-4195-3580-2
  ISBN-10: 1-4195-3580-3
  1. Real property—United States—Dictionaries. 2. Real estate business—Law and legislation—United States—Dictionaries. I. Spodek, Marie S. II. Title.
  KF568.5.R445 2006
  346.7304'603--dc22
                                        2006008387

Contents

A

A, B, C, D paper Categorization of borrower and loans in order of risk based on credit scores.

abandonment The act of voluntarily surrendering or relinquishing possession of real property without vesting this interest in any other person.

abatement A reduction or decrease in amount, degree, intensity, or worth.

able Refers to financial ability in the phrase "ready, willing, and able buyer," used to determine whether a broker is entitled to a commission.

absentee owner A property owner who does not reside on the property and who often relies on a property manager to manage the investment.

absolute Unrestricted and without conditions or limitations, as in a fee simple absolute estate or an absolute conveyance or absolute liability (strict liability).

absorption rate An estimate of the rate at which a particular classification of space—such as new office space, new housing, or new condominium units—will be sold or occupied each year.

abstracter One who prepares an abstract of title. Also spelled *abstractor*. (See **abstract of title**)

abstracter's certificate A warranty by an abstracter that an abstract contains all matters of public record affecting title to a specific tract of land. (See **abstract of title**)

abstract of judgment Document used to effectuate a judgment lien. Must be filed in any county where the judgment debtor has real estate. (See **attachment, general lien, judgment lien, lis pendens**)

abstract of title A full summary of all consecutive grants, conveyances, wills, records, and judicial proceedings affecting title to a specific parcel of real estate, together with a statement of all recorded liens and encumbrances affecting the property and their present status.

acceleration clause A provision in a mortgage, trust deed, promissory note, or contract for deed (agreement of sale) that, upon the occurrence of a specified event, gives the lender (payee, obligee, or mortgagee) the right to call all sums due and payable in advance of the fixed payment date.

acceptance The expression of intent of a person receiving an offer (offeree, such as the seller in a real estate transaction) to be bound by the terms of the offer that must be communicated to the person making the offer (offeror, such as a buyer).

access A means by which property is approached or a method of entrance into or upon a property; also a general or specific right of ingress and egress to a particular property.

accessibility The relative ease of entry to a site and its location with respect to different transportation facilities; also, the ability of a person with a handicap or disability to more easily and independently approach and use facilities.

accession The acquisition of title to additional land or to improvements as a result of the annexation of fixtures or as a result of alluvial deposits along the banks of streams by accretion.

accord and satisfaction The settlement of an obligation that is something different from or less than what the creditor feels he or she is entitled to.

accounting The fiduciary duty of an agent to maintain and preserve the property and money of the principal.

account payable A liability (debt) representing an amount owed to a creditor, usually arising from the purchase of merchandise, supplies, or services.

account receivable A claim against a debtor, usually arising from sales or services rendered to the debtor. The opposite of an account payable, an account receivable is not necessarily due or past due at any specific time.

accretion The gradual and imperceptible addition of land by alluvial deposits of soil through natural causes, such as shoreline movement caused by streams or rivers.

accrual method An accounting method of reporting income and expenses in which expenses incurred and income earned for a given period are reported whether or not the expenses were paid or income was received.

accrued Accumulated over a period of time, such as accrued depreciation, accrued interest, or accrued expenses.

A

accrued depreciation
1. In accounting, a bookkeeping account that shows the total amount of depreciation taken on an asset since it was acquired.
2. For appraisal purposes, the difference between the cost to reproduce the property (as of the appraisal date) and the property's current value as judged by its "competitive condition."

acknowledgment A formal declaration made before a duly authorized officer, usually a notary public, by a person who has signed a document, confirming that the signature is voluntary and genuine; also, the document itself.

STATE OF: SS:

COUNTY OF:

On this _____ day of _____, 20___,
before me personally appeared _____,
to me known to be the person(s) described in and who executed
the foregoing instrument and acknowledged to me that _____
executed the same as _____ free act and deed.

                                _____

                                Notary Public
(NOTARY SEAL)

                                My Commission Expires: _____

---

acquired immunodeficiency syndrome (AIDS) A serious disease of the immune system. Persons with acquired immunodeficiency syndrome are protected under most federal and state discrimination laws.

acquisition cost The amount of money or other valuable consideration expended to obtain title to property.

acre (AC) A measure of land area equal to 43,560 square feet or 208.71 feet by 208.71 feet.

act of God An act of nature beyond human control, such as a tidal wave, flood, hurricane, volcanic eruption, or earthquake.

actual age The chronological age of a building; the opposite of its effective age, as indicated by the building's condition and utility.

actual cash value An insurance term for the monetary worth of an improvement calculated by subtracting the value of the physical wear of a property from its replacement cost.

actual damages Those damages that a court of law recognizes and that are a direct result of a wrong.

actual eviction The process of physically removing a tenant after the court issues a judgment decree for possession in favor of the owner and the tenant does not voluntarily leave. (See **eviction**)

actual notice Express information or fact; that which is known; actual knowledge.

actuary A person usually associated with an insurance company or savings and loan association, and skilled in calculating the value of life interests, pension plans, and annuities.

A

ADA See **Americans with Disabilities Act (ADA).**

adaptability The ability at a later date to change easily physical designs in residential or commercial units to accommodate needs for those encountering mobility limitations.

addendum Additional material attached to and made part of a document.

addition Any construction that increases a building's size or significantly adds to it.

additional deposit The additional earnest money given by the buyer to the seller or to escrow under a purchase agreement.

adhesion contract A contract in which one of the parties may only accept or reject the contract but may not negotiate any portion of it; an insurance contract. Any ambiguity is usually construed in favor of the party who did not write the contract.

adjustable-rate loan A broad term for a loan (mortgage or deed of trust) with rates and terms that can change. The adjustable-rate loan has created its own glossary of terms, such as:

> *Current index:* The current value of a recognized index as calculated and published nationally or regionally and its changes used to calculate the new note rate as of each rate adjustment date.

> *Fully indexed note rate:* The index value at the time of application plus the gross margin stated in the note.

Gross margin: An amount, expressed as percentage points, added to the current index value on the rate adjustment date to establish the new note rate.

Initial rate: The below-market rate charged for the first adjustment period to attract borrowers (the "teaser rate").

Initial rate discount: The index value at the time of loan application plus the gross margin minus the initial note rate.

Life of loan cap: A ceiling that the note rate cannot exceed over the life of the loan.

Note rate: The rate that determines the amount of annual interest charged to the borrower.

Payment adjustment date: The date on which the borrower's monthly principal and interest payment may change.

Payment cap: A limit on the amount of increase in the borrower's monthly principal and interest at the payment adjustment date.

Payment rate: The rate at which the borrower repays the loan.

Periodic interest rate cap: A limit on the increase or decrease in the note rate at each rate adjustment.

Rate adjustment date: The date on which the borrower's note rate may change.

A

adjustable-rate mortgage (ARM)   See **adjustable-rate loan**.

adjusted basis The original cost basis of a property reduced by certain deductions and increased by certain improvement costs.

adjustment interval The frequency with which the interest rate and the monthly payment amount can be reset in an adjustable-rate mortgage loan.

adjustments
1. In appraisal, the increases or decreases to the sales price of a comparable property to arrive at an indicated value for the property being appraised.
2. In real estate closings, the credits and debits of a settlement statement such as real property tax, insurance, and rent prorations.

administrative law judge In the United States, the administrative law judge (ALJ) is the presiding officer who conducts administrative hearings at which the parties present evidence.

administrative regulations Regulations issued by an administrative agency, which have the force and effect of law.

administrator A person appointed by the court to settle the estate of a person who has died intestate (leaving no will).

ad valorem Latin for "according to valuation," usually referring to a type of tax or assessment.

advance To give consideration before it is due.

A

adverse possession The acquiring of title to real property owned by someone else by means of open, notorious, hostile, and continuous possession for a statutory period of time.

adverse use The prescriptive acquisition of the right to a limited use of another's land; for example, a pathway easement across another's property.

advertising The public promotion of one's products and services, and real estate, governed by various rules and regulations established by federal, state, local, and private authorities.

affidavit A sworn statement written and made under oath before a notary public or other official authorized by law to administer an oath.

STATE OF: SS:
COUNTY OF:

_____ being duly sworn, deposes and says
that (he) is the _____ of _____,
      (she)
the applicant named in the foregoing application, and that the
statements made in the application are true and correct
to the best of (his) knowledge and belief.
               (her)

_____
                (signature)
Subscribed and sworn to before me this
_____ day of _____, 20_____
Notary Public
My Commission Expires: _____

---

affidavit of title (affidavit of ownership) A written statement made under oath by the seller or grantor and acknowledged before a notary public.

A

affiliate broker See **associate broker**.

affirmation A declaration as to the truth of a statement, used in lieu of an oath, especially when the affiant or deponent objects to taking an oath for personal or religious reasons.

affirmative marketing program A program designed to inform proactively all buyers in a minority community of homes for sale without discrimination and to provide real estate licensees with procedures and educational materials to assist in compliance with the law.

affordability index A standard established by the National Association of REALTORS® to gauge the financial ability of consumers to buy a home.

affordable housing Housing for individuals or families whose incomes are a certain percentage of or below the median for the area as determined by HUD and adjusted for family size.

after-tax income In accounting, the amount left after deducting income tax liability from taxable income.

agency A relationship created when one person, the *principal,* delegates to another, the *agent,* the right to act on his or her behalf in business transactions and to exercise some degree of discretion while so acting.

agency by ratification An agency created "after the fact" by a principal expressly or impliedly affirming the conduct of a party claiming to act as his or her agent.

agency coupled with an interest An agency relationship in which the agent acquires an estate or interest in the subject of the agency (the property).

agent One authorized to represent and to act on behalf of another person (called the principal).

aggrieved Having suffered loss or injury from infringement or denial of rights.

agreement of sale The terms that set up the transfer ownership from one owner to another.

AIDS See **acquired immunodeficiency syndrome.**

air rights Rights to the use of the open space or vertical plane above a property.

air space In condominium ownership, what is actually owned by the unit owner (in addition to tenancy in common for the common areas).

aleatory contract A contract that depends on a contingency or uncertain event, such as a fire insurance contract or a lottery agreement. (See **contract**)

alien A person born outside the jurisdiction of the United States who has not been naturalized under the Constitution and U.S. laws and is not a citizen of the United States.

alienation The act of transferring ownership, title, or an interest or estate in real property from one person to another.

alienation clause A provision sometimes found in a promissory note or mortgage that provides that the balance of the secured debt becomes immediately due and payable at the option of the

A

mortgagee upon the alienation of the property by the mortgagor.

allodial system An estate holding the potential of existing indefinitely, with free and full ownership of rights in land by individuals, which is the basis of real property law in the United States.

allotment The funds allocated for the purchase of mortgages within a specified time by a permanent investor with whom a mortgage loan originator has a relationship but not a specific contract in the form of a commitment.

all-risks policy Previously, a term used to describe a homeowner's insurance policy, now replaced by the term *special form* which includes coverage for all direct physical damage not otherwise excluded.

alluvion The material that constitutes the increase of soil on a shore or riverbank, added by the process of accretion.

amenities Features, both tangible and intangible, which enhance and add to the value or desirability of real estate.

Americans with Disabilities Act (ADA) A federal law, effective in 1992, designed to eliminate discrimination against individuals with disabilities by mandating equal access to jobs, public accommodations, government services, public transportation, and telecommunications.

amortization Self-liquidating (literally, "killing-off"). The gradual repayment or retiring of a debt by means of systematic payments of principal and/or interest over a set period, so that at the end of the period there is a zero balance.

amortization schedule A table showing the amounts of principal and interest due at regular intervals and the unpaid balance of the loan after each payment.

Monthly Amortized Payments
Term (Years)

Amount	5	10	15	20	25	30	35
$39,000	$809.67	$494.08	$395.59	$350.91	$307.30	$313.81	$305.76
40,000	830.43	506.75	405.73	359.91	335.68	321.86	313.60
41,000	851.19	519.42	415.88	368.91	344.08	329.90	321.44

ancestor A person from whom one lineally descends (such as a father or grandmother) and from whom land is lawfully inherited.

anchor tenant A major department or chain store strategically located at a shopping center so as to give maximum exposure to smaller, satellite stores.

angle A measure of rotation around a point, generally used in surveys to show the relationship of one line to another.

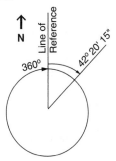

A

annexation An addition to property by the act of joining or uniting one thing to another, as in attaching personal property to real property and thereby creating a fixture.

annual debt service The amount of money required on an annual basis for payment of interest and principal on all security interests on the real property (for example, mortgages, deeds of trust, and contracts for deed).

annual exclusion for gift tax An amount of gift income that the donor may exclude from gift taxation.

annual meeting A yearly meeting of shareholders of a corporation or members of an association held for the purpose of permitting them to vote on the election of directors and various other matters of corporate or association business.

annual percentage rate (APR) An expression of the relationship of the total finance charge to the total amount to be financed as required under the federal Truth-in-Lending Act.

annual report A statement of the financial status and progress of a corporation during its previous fiscal year, usually containing a balance sheet, operating statement, and auditor's report.

annuity A sum of money received by the annuitant at fixed intervals as one of a series of periodic payments.

antenuptial agreement A contract entered into by two people contemplating marriage for the purpose of settling the property rights of both in advance, also called a prenuptial ("prenup").

anticipatory breach A declaration of intention not to perform made by a buyer or seller through words or acts prior to closing at which time the other party, not being in default, is entitled to enforce the contract in court without first having to offer or tender performance.

antitrust laws State and federal laws designed to maintain and preserve business competition prohibiting price fixing, certain types of boycotts, allocation of customers or markets, restrictions on competition in shopping center leases, and certain restraints placed on franchisees by franchisors.

apartment building A building having separate units for permanent tenants who rent or lease them.

appeal
1. The process under law of taking a case decision to a higher court to seek review, reversal, or retrial of the case.
2. The legal process by which a property owner may challenge a property tax assessment.

apportionment
1. The division or partition of property into proportionate (though not necessarily equal) parts.
2. The pro rata division of real estate carrying charges between buyer and seller at closing.

A

appraisal The process of developing and communicating an opinion about a property's value in one of three ways: direct sales comparison approach, cost approach, and income approach.

appraiser One who estimates value.

appreciation A temporary or permanent increase in the worth or value of property due to economic causes.

appurtenance Those things belonging to the property, but not for all time; all those rights, privileges, and improvements that belong to and pass with the transfer of property but are not necessarily a part of the actual property.

appurtenant Belonging to; adjunctive; appended or annexed to.

arbitrage
1. The spread, or difference, between interest rates; a common item in all-inclusive or wraparound mortgage financing.
2. The simultaneous purchase and sale of mortgages or mortgage-backed securities in different markets to profit from price differentials.

arbitration The nonjudicial submission of a controversy to selected third parties for their determination in a manner provided by agreement or by law.

area A parcel of land assumed to be level and at sea level.

arm's-length transaction A transaction in which the parties are dealing from equal bargaining positions.

arranger of credit As defined under the federal Truth-in-Lending Act, a person who regularly arranges for the extension of consumer credit by another person if a finance charge will be imposed, if there are to be more than four installments, and if the person extending the credit is not a creditor.

arrears
1. The state of being delinquent in paying a debt.
2. At or after the end of the period for which expenses are due or levied; the opposite of in advance.

articles of incorporation The document that sets forth the purposes, powers, and basic rules of operation for a corporation.

asbestos A fire-resistant mineral fiber not easily destroyed or degraded by natural processes; previously used extensively in building materials but now avoided because it causes cancer in those working with asbestos-containing materials.

asbestos-containing materials (ACMs) Materials that contain asbestos and classified as either nonfriable (sheathed and/or crumbling) or the more dangerous friable, easily crumbled by hand pressure.

"as is" Words in a contract intended to signify that the seller offers the property in its present condition, with no modifications or improvements, and serves as a disclaimer of warranties or representations.

A

asking price The listed price of a parcel of real estate—the price at which it is offered to the public by the seller or broker.

assemblage The combining of two or more adjoining lots into one large tract.

assessed valuation The value of real property established for the purpose of computing real property taxes.

assessment
1. An official valuation of real property for tax purposes based on appraisals by local government officials.
2. The allocation of the proportionate individual share of a common expense, as when the owners of condominium or cooperative units are assessed for their proportionate share of unusual maintenance expenses for the buildings that benefit the project as a whole and are not funded through regular maintenance charges.
3. A specific levy for a definite purpose, such as adding curbs or sewers in a neighborhood.
4. An official determination of the just compensation a property owner should be paid for the taking of his or her property for a public purpose (condemnation).
5. An additional capital contribution of corporate shareholders or members of a partnership or association to cover a capital expenditure.

assessment rolls Public records of the assessed values of all lands and buildings within a specific area.

A

assessor A public official who appraises property for tax purposes.

asset Something of value owned by a person; a useful item of property.

asset depreciation range system (ADR) The part of the Internal Revenue Service regulations covering guidelines and standards for determining the period over which to depreciate an asset.

assignment The transfer of the right, title, and interest in the property of one person (the assignor) to another (the assignee).

assignment of lease The transfer of all title, right, and interest that a lessee possesses in certain real property.

assignment of rents An agreement between a property owner and a mortgagee by which the mortgagee receives, as security, the right to collect rents from the mortgagor's tenants, although the mortgagor continues to have the sole obligation to the tenants under the lease. (See **foreclosure**)

associate broker A real estate license classification used in some states to describe a person who has qualified as a real estate broker but still works for and is supervised by another broker; also called a **broker-salesperson, broker-associate,** or **affiliate broker.**

associate licensee Another name for a licensed real estate salesperson.

association A group of people gathered together for a business purpose, sometimes treated as a corporation under tax law.

association of unit owners All unit owners of a condominium acting as a group for the administration of the project, in accordance with the declaration and bylaws.

assumption of mortgage The acts of acquiring title to property that has an existing mortgage and agreeing to be personally liable for the terms and conditions of the mortgage, including payments.

at-risk rules Special rules set up by the Internal Revenue Service to restrict leverage opportunity by limiting the taxpayer's deductible losses to the amount he or she has "at risk." A taxpayer is generally considered at risk to the extent of cash contributed and amounts borrowed for which he or she is liable for payment from personal assets (recourse debt).

attachment The legal process of seizing the real or personal property of a defendant in a lawsuit by levy or judicial order, and holding it in court custody as security for satisfaction of a judgment.

attorney-in-fact A competent and disinterested person who is authorized by another person to act in his or her place.

attractive nuisance A doctrine of tort law stating that a person who maintains on his or her property a condition that is both dangerous and conceivably inviting to children owes a duty to exercise reasonable care to protect children from the danger.

auction A form of selling land or personal property whereby oral offers are taken and the property is sold to the highest bidder. (See **bid, online auction**)

authorization to sell A listing contract whereby a seller employs an agent to procure a buyer for the property.

avulsion The loss of land as a result of its being washed away by a sudden or violent action of nature, not usually resulting in losing title to the land lost by this sudden action.

B

back-to-back escrow An escrow set up to handle the concurrent sale of one property and the purchase of another property by the same party.

back-to-back lease An agreement made by a landlord as a concession to a prospective tenant, in which the landlord agrees to take over the tenant's existing lease in return for the tenant's agreement to lease space in the landlord's commercial building (office building, industrial park).

backup offer An offer to buy submitted to a seller with the understanding that the seller has already accepted a prior offer; a secondary offer.

balance sheet An itemized financial statement setting forth personal or corporate assets, liabilities, and net worth (the difference between assets and liabilities) as of a specified date.

balloon payment Under an installment obligation, a final payment that is substantially larger than the previous installment payments and repays the debt in full; the remaining balance that is due at the maturity of a note or at obligation time.

bankruptcy A condition of financial insolvency in which a person's liabilities exceed assets and the person is unable to pay current debts; may be voluntary or involuntary, and may be a stated ground for default under a lease or contract for deed.

bargain and sale deed A deed, formerly in the form of a contract between buyer and seller, that recites a consideration and conveys all of the grantor's interest in the property to the grantee which usually does not include warranties as to the title of the property conveyed.

base line One of a set of imaginary lines running east and west used by surveyors for reference in locating and describing land under the government survey method of property description.

base period A time interval or starting point used for calculating certain business and economic data, frequently found in escalation clauses, often of great significance in commercial leases.

base rent The minimum rental stipulated under a percentage lease. The first year is called the *base year* and each succeeding year is called a *comparison year.*

basis The dollar amount that the Internal Revenue Service attributes to an asset for purposes of determining annual depreciation or cost recovery, and gain or loss on the sale of the asset.

beach Land on the margin of a sea, lake, or river.

bench mark A permanent reference mark (PRM) affixed to a durable object, such as an iron post or brass marker embedded in a sidewalk, used to establish elevations and altitudes above sea level over a surveyed area; also used in tidal observation.

benchmark
1. The standard or base from which specific estimates are made.
2. A major court decision that serves as the precedent or guideline for future decisions.

beneficiary A person who receives benefits from the gifts or acts of another, as in the case of one designated to receive the proceeds from a will, insurance policy, or trust; the real owner, as opposed to the trustee, who holds only legal title.

betterment An improvement to real property, such as a sidewalk or road, which substantially increases the property's value.

bid
1. An offer to purchase property for a specified amount, such as at an auction, foreclosure, or probate sale.
2. Formal procedure of submission, by a list of contract bidders, of sealed proposals to perform certain work at a cost specified in the proposal, usually within a set period of time.

bilateral contract A contract in which each party promises to perform an act in exchange for the other party's promise to perform, such as a real estate sales contract.

bill of sale A written agreement by which one person sells, assigns, or transfers to another his or her right to, or interest in, personal property.

binder
1. An agreement formed by the receipt of an earnest money deposit for the purchase of real property as evidence of the purchaser's good faith and intention to complete the transaction
2. A written instrument giving immediate fire and extended insurance coverage until a regular insurance policy can be issued, sometimes obtained pending the closing of a real estate transaction.

3. A temporary contract of title insurance in which the insurer agrees to issue a specified policy within a certain period of time.

biweekly payment loan A loan that calls for 26 half-month payments a year, resulting in an earlier loan retirement date and lower total interest costs than with a typical fully amortized loan with regular monthly payments.

blanket mortgage A mortgage secured by several properties or a number of lots; often used to secure construction financing for proposed subdivisions or condominium development projects and containing a "partial release" clause to obtain a release from the blanket mortgage for each lot as it is sold.

blind ad An advertisement that does not include the name and address of the person placing the ad, only a phone number or post office box address. Licensed brokers are generally prohibited by state license laws from using blind ads.

blockbusting An illegal and discriminatory practice whereby one person induces another to enter into a real estate transaction from which the first person may benefit financially by representing that a change may occur in the neighborhood with respect to race, sex, religion, color, handicap, familial status, or ancestry of the occupants, a change possibly resulting in the lowering of the property values, a decline in the quality of schools, or an increase in the crime rate; also known as panic selling.

B

blue book One of any number of handy reference books that lists new and used values.

board of directors The governing body of a corporation authorized to carry on and control the business affairs of the company, the members of which are elected periodically by shareholders.

boilerplate The standard, fixed language in a contract, such as that found in most mortgages, contracts of sale, contracts for deed, leases, and CC&Rs (covenants, conditions, and restrictions).

BOMA *Building Owners and Managers Association*. See Appendix A.

bona fide purchaser (BFP) One who acquires property in good faith and for a valuable consideration without knowledge, actual or constructive, of the prior rights or equities of third parties.

bond A written promise that generally accompanies a mortgage and is the primary evidence of the debt obligation secured by the mortgage; may also refer to a completion bond or a performance bond. (See **performance bond**)

bonus depreciation See **first-year depreciation**.

book value The amount at which an asset is carried on the financial books of a person, partnership, association, or corporation.

boot Money or other property that is not like-kind, given to make up any difference in value or equity between exchanged properties.

B

boundaries The perimeters or limits of a parcel of land as fixed by legal description.

branch office Any secondary place of business apart from the principal or main office from which real estate business is conducted.

breach of contract Any violation of the terms or conditions of a contract without legal excuse; default; nonperformance.

break-even point In residential or commercial property, the figure at which rental income is equal to all required expenses and debt service.

bridge loan A short-term loan to cover the period between the termination of one loan, such as an interim construction loan, and the beginning of another loan, such as a permanent takeout loan; the loan between the acquisition of a property and its improvement or development to make it qualify for a permanent loan.

British thermal unit (Btu) A unit of measure of heat, used in rating the capacity of air-conditioning and heating equipment (radiators, boilers).

broker One who acts as an intermediary between parties to a transaction. A real estate broker is a properly licensed party (individual, corporation, or partnership) who, for a valuable consideration or promise of consideration, serves as a special agent to others to facilitate the sale or lease of real property.

brokerage The aspect of the real estate business that is concerned with bringing together the parties and completing a real estate transaction involving exchanges, rentals, and trade-ins of property, as well as sales.

broker-dealer One licensed to buy and sell securities.

broker-in-charge In many states, a broker designated by the principal broker of a real estate brokerage company and registered with the state real estate license commission as the person directly in charge of, and responsible to, the principal broker for the real estate operations conducted at a branch office.

broker price opinion (BPO) A broker's written opinion of the value of a particular property that may not be used in connection with originating a federally related loan; not an appraisal.

brownfields Industrial properties in which the expansion, redevelopment, or reuse may be complicated by the presence or potential presence of a hazardous substance, pollutant, or contaminant.

budget A balance sheet or statement of estimated receipts and expenditures.

budget mortgage A mortgage with payments set up to cover more than interest and principal reductions, usually including $\frac{1}{12}$ of the year's property taxes, a pro rata share of the fire insurance premium (together known as *PITI*), and any other similar charges that if not paid, could result in a foreclosure.

buffer zone In zoning, a strip of land separating one land use from another.

builder's risk insurance Fire, liability, and extended-coverage insurance written to cover the special risks of a building under construction.

building codes Rules set up by local, state, or municipal governments to regulate building and construction standards by providing minimum standards to safeguard the health, safety, and welfare of the public.

building line A setback line; a line beyond which one may not build any improvement.

building permit A written governmental permission for the construction of a new building or other improvement, the demolition or substantial repair of an existing structure, or the installation of factory-built housing.

building related illness (BRI) A clinically diagnosed condition that is caused by toxic substances or pathogens that persist when an occupant leaves the building.

building restrictions Limitations on the size or types of improvements established by zoning acts or by private restrictions inserted in a deed or ground lease.

building standards The specific elements of construction the owner/developer chooses to provide tenants with throughout a building.

build-to-suit An understanding or contract in which a lessor agrees to develop a property or finish certain space to the specifications of a lessee in return for a lease commitment on the part of the prospective tenant.

built-ins Certain stationary equipment—such as some kitchen appliances, bookcases, desks, shelving, cabinets, and furniture—permanently affixed to real property and understood to be included when the property is sold.

bundle of rights An ownership concept describing all the legal rights that attach to the ownership of real property, including the right to sell, lease, encumber, use, enjoy, exclude, and devise by will.

burden of proof The obligation to prove the truth or falsity of a fact, in either a trial or an administrative hearing.

business day A day of the week, except Saturdays, Sundays, and holidays; a normal working day.

business interruption insurance Insurance that covers losses incurred as a result of a business owner's inability to conduct business during the repair of a building following a fire or other insured hazard.

business opportunity The sale or lease of the business and goodwill of an existing business, enterprise, or opportunity, including a sale of all or substantially all of the assets or stock of a corporation, or assets of a partnership or sole proprietorship.

business park A development or subdivision designed for office-warehouse or like use, also known as an *office park*.

buy-back agreement A provision in a sales contract that provides that the seller (and, in some cases, the broker) will buy back the property within a specified period, usually for the original selling price, upon the happening of a certain event.

buydown A financing technique used to reduce the monthly payment for the home-buying borrower during the initial years, often employed by builders willing to reduce their profit on the sale or by adding part of this cost of doing business to the price of the home.

buyer's broker A broker who represents the buyer in a fiduciary capacity.

buyer's market An economic situation in which the supply of properties available for sale exceeds the demand, resulting in a decline in prices.

buy-sell agreement An agreement among partners or shareholders to the effect that one party will sell and another party will buy a business interest at a stated price upon the occurrence of a stated event.

bylaws The regulations, rules, or laws adopted by a condominium owners' association or corporation for the condominium's management and operation.

C

cancellation clause A clause in a lease that may permit the lessor or the lessee the right to terminate the lease term upon the happening of certain stated events or occurrences by the payment from one party to the other of definite amounts of money as consideration.

cap A ceiling or limit on the adjustments made in the payments, interest rate, or balance of an adjustable-rate loan.

capacity of parties The legal ability of people or organizations to enter into a valid contract; the parties have full, limited, or no capacity to contract.

capital That money and/or property comprising the wealth owned or used by a person or business enterprise; the accumulated wealth of a person or business.

capital assets All property except that held by a taxpayer primarily for sale to customers in the ordinary course of one's trade or business.

capital expenditure The cost of a capital improvement that extends the life of the asset.

capital gain The taxable profit derived from the sale of a capital asset.

C

capital improvement Any structure erected as a permanent improvement to real property; any improvement made to extend the useful life of a property or to add to the value of the property.

capitalization A mathematical process for converting net income into an indication of value, commonly used in the income approach to value.

capitalization (CAP) rate The percentage selected for use in the income approach to valuation of improved property. Reflects the recapture of the original investment over the economic life of the improvement to give investors an acceptable rate of return (yield) on their original investments and to provide for the return of the invested equity.

capitalize To provide cash; to fund.

capital loss A loss derived from the sale of a capital asset, such as securities, stocks, or bonds.

caravan In some parts of the country, a group inspection tour of listed properties by a broker's sales staff.

carryback financing Financing in which the seller takes back a note for part of the purchase price secured by a junior mortgage (a second or third mortgage), wraparound mortgage, or contract for deed.

carrying charges

1. The regular costs of maintaining a property, such as taxes, insurance, utilities, and accrued interest.

2. Costs incurred in owning property up to the time the development of the property is completed.

cash equivalency An adjustment made to a comparable property sale that was financed in a manner not typical of the marketplace.

cash flow The spendable income from an investment after deducting from gross income all operating and fixed expenses, including principal and interest.

cash-flow statement A yearly financial report showing the bottom-line return after taxes.

cashier's check A bill of exchange (check) drawn by a bank (usually signed by its cashier) upon itself as drawer and payable upon demand, like a promissory note executed by the bank.

cash method An accounting method of reporting income in the taxable year in which the income is actually or constructively received and reporting expenses when actually paid out.

cash on cash The before-tax cash flow divided by the capital invested in the property; a method to determine how efficiently capital invested in the property is used.

cause of action Facts or circumstances that give rise to a right to file a lawsuit.

caveat emptor Latin for "let the buyer beware." A buyer should inspect the goods or realty before purchase, because the buyer buys "as is" and at his or her own risk.

cease and desist order An order from a government authority directing a person violating the law to refrain from continuing to do so.

cemetery lots A special land-use designation created when the landowner or cemetery authority dedicates property exclusively to cemetery use.

central business district (CBD) A city's downtown area in which is concentrated the main business, governmental, recreational, professional, and service activities of the community.

certificate of eligibility A certificate issued by a Department of Veterans Affairs regional office to veterans who qualify for a VA loan.

certificate of insurance A certificate in which an insurance company verifies that a particular policy insuring certain parties is in effect for given amounts. Often required in commercial leases requiring the lessee to maintain certain specified insurance coverage.

certificate of no defense
  1. A legal instrument executed by a mortgagor setting forth the exact unpaid balance of a mortgage, the current rate of interest, and the date to which interest has been paid, also called an estoppel certificate.
  2. In a landlord-tenant situation, a certificate of no defense is a statement by the tenant setting forth the amount of rent payable and the term of the lease and acknowledging that the tenant claims no defenses or offsets against the landlord,

C

sometimes required when the landlord is selling the property or is assigning the lease.

certificate of occupancy (CO) A certificate issued by a governmental authority indicating that a building is ready and fit for occupancy and that there are no building code violations.

certificate of reasonable value (CRV) A certificate issued by the Department of Veterans Affairs setting forth a property's current market value estimate, based on a VA-approved appraisal.

certificate of title A statement of opinion prepared by a title company, licensed abstracter, or an attorney on the status of a title to a parcel of real property, based on an examination of specified public records.

certified appraiser Under the provisions of FIRREA, an appraiser who has been certified (licensed) by the appropriate state agency to value real property in that state.

certified check A check that the issuer (usually a bank) guarantees to be good, and against which a stop payment directive is ineffective if the payee obtains the certification.

certified copy A copy of a document (such as a deed, marriage, or birth certificate) signed by the person having possession of the original and declaring it to be a true copy.

certify To testify in writing; to confirm; to guarantee in writing, as in a certified check; to endorse, as with a proper seal.

C

chain of title The recorded history of matters that affect the title to a specific parcel of real property, such as ownership, encumbrances, and liens, usually beginning with the original recorded source of the title, showing the successive changes of ownership, each one linked to the next so that a "chain" is formed.

change order An order to a contractor from the owner, architect, or engineer on a construction project authorizing changes or modifications to the original work as shown in the contract drawings, plans, or specifications.

chattel An item of tangible personal property.

chattel mortgage A mortgage secured by personal property.

check A negotiable instrument signed by a maker or drawer authorizing a bank to pay money to the payee or bearer.

churning The practice of transferring property to gain some advantage.

Civil Rights Act of 1866 A federal act that prohibits *all* racial discrimination, affirmed in 1968, in *Jones v. Alfred H. Mayer Company.*

Civil Rights Acts 1968 See **federal fair housing law**.

Clayton Antitrust Act Federal statute passed in 1914 to clarify and supplement the Sherman Antitrust Act of 1890 by defining varied types of illegal business practices and prohibiting exclusive sales contracts, local price cutting to freeze out competitors, certain rebates, and certain corporate acquisitions of stock and interlocking directorates.

clearing title The process of examining all recorded and unrecorded instruments affecting a particular property and taking any necessary action to remove or otherwise cure the title of any defects or clouds in order that the title may become a good, marketable title.

clear title Title to property that is free from liens, defects, or other encumbrances, except those the buyer has agreed to accept, such as a mortgage to be assumed or a restriction of record; established title; title without clouds.

client The person who employs an agent to perform a service for a fee; also called a principal.

client trust account An account set up by a broker to keep a client's monies segregated from the broker's general funds; also called an earnest money account.

closed-end mortgage A mortgage that prohibits the mortgagor from using the property as security for further loans.

closed mortgage A "lock-in" mortgage; one that cannot be prepaid during a specified period of time or until maturity.

closing (settlement) The consummation of a real estate transaction, when the seller delivers title to the buyer in exchange for payment by the buyer of the purchase price.

closing agent A neutral third party responsible for assembling documents for the transfer of real property.

closing costs Expenses of the sale (or loan refinancing) that must be paid in addition to the purchase price (in the case of the buyer's expenses) or be deducted from the proceeds of the sale (in the case of the seller's expenses).

closing statement A detailed cash accounting of a real estate transaction prepared by a broker, escrow officer, attorney, or other person designated to process the mechanics of the sale, showing all cash received, all charges and credits made, and all cash paid out in the transaction; a HUD-1 form.

cloud on title Any document, claim, unreleased lien, or encumbrance that may superficially impair or injure the title to a property or cast doubt on the title's validity, often revealed by a title search.

cluster development The grouping of housing units on less-than-normal-size home sites, with remaining land used as common areas.

cluster zoning A zoning provision whereby a specific residential or unit density is prescribed for an entire area with flexible site-planning criteria that differs from traditional zoning ordinances that allocate zoning on a lot-by-lot basis.

Code of Ethics A written system of standards of ethical conduct.

codicil A supplement or addition to a will that normally does not revoke the entire will.

C

coinsurance A common provision in hazard insurance policies under which the insured agrees to maintain insurance in an amount equal to at least 80 percent of the replacement cost; if not, in the event of a loss, the insurance company will make the insured share in the loss on a pro rata basis.

cold call An unsolicited inquiry from a real estate office or salesperson to a prospective buyer or seller, a way to introduce the company or salesperson to a prospect.

cold canvass Obtaining listings by door-to-door solicitation of homeowners.

collateral Something of value given or pledged as security for a debt or obligation.

collateralized mortgage A loan secured by collateral in addition to real estate, as with a pledged savings account.

collection account An account established by someone to receive periodic payments on a debt or obligation, to make disbursements as requested by the payee and to make an accounting to both parties, often used in wraparound mortgage situations.

color of title A condition in which a title appears to be good, but because of a certain defect, it is in fact invalid (paper title).

commencement of work The noticeable beginning of an improvement on real estate as determined under local law having significance relative to the effective date of a mechanic's lien (and thus the priority against other liens such as mortgages), as well as protecting a builder against changes in the zoning rules.

commercial property A classification of real estate that includes income-producing property such as office buildings, gasoline stations, restaurants, shopping centers, hotels and motels, parking lots, and stores.

commingling To mingle or mix; for example, to deposit client funds in the broker's personal or general account, which is generally prohibited.

commission The compensation paid to a real estate broker (usually by the seller) for services rendered in connection with the sale or exchange of real property.

commissioner A member of a state regulatory real estate commission, board, or division.

commitment A pledge or promise to do a certain act, such as the promise of a lending institution to loan a certain amount of money at a specified rate of interest to a qualified buyer, provided the loan is made by a certain date.

common area maintenance Fees charged directly to tenants by owners for upkeep of common areas.

common areas Land or improvements in a condominium development designated for the use and benefit of all residents, property owners, and tenants.

common elements Parts of a property that are necessary or convenient to the existence, maintenance, and safety of a condominium, or are normally in common use by all of the condominium residents.

common expenses The operating expenses of condominium common elements, together with all other sums designated as common expenses by or pursuant to the condominium declaration or bylaws.

common interest The percentage of undivided ownership in the common elements belonging to each condominium apartment, as established in the condominium declaration.

common law That body of law based on usage, general acceptance, and custom, as manifested in decrees and judgments of the courts; judge-made law ("case law") as opposed to codified or statutory law (or civil law as found in a few states like Louisiana).

common profits

1. In a condominium, the balance of all income, rents, profits, and revenues from the common elements remaining after the deduction of the common expenses.
2. The profits derived from the operations of a partnership or corporation.

common wall A wall separating two living units in a condominium project.

community property A system of property ownership based on the theory that each spouse has an equal interest in the property acquired by the efforts of either spouse during marriage. Community states do not recognize dower, curtesy, and survivorship rights.

community shopping center A shopping center of approximately 150,000 square feet and 20 to 70 retail spaces, which is classified between the smaller neighborhood center and the larger regional center and supported by more than 5,000 families.

comparables Recently sold or leased properties that are similar to a particular property being evaluated and are used to indicate a value for the subject property.

comparative unit method A method used to determine the reproduction cost in which all components of a building are added together on a unit basis, such as cost per square foot.

compensatory damages The damages awarded to the plaintiff by a court, intended to cover the actual injury or economic loss, not including punitive damages or damages for grossly negligent behavior.

competent party A party to a contract who possesses the legal capacity to enter into a binding contract.

competitive market analysis (CMA) A tool used by brokers and salespeople to assist consumers in determining a property's sale price consisting of information about three types of properties similar to the subject property: those sold, on the market, and listings that expired. It is not an appraisal

complainant A person who makes a complaint or instigates legal action against another (the respondent).

completion bond A surety bond posted by a landowner or developer to guarantee that a proposed development will be completed according to specifications, free and clear of all mechanics' liens.

compliance inspection
1. Inspection by a public official of a structure to ensure its compliance with all building codes and specifications.
2. Inspection of a construction site or structure by either a lending institution (for a conventional mortgage loan) or a government representative (for an FHA or VA loan) to ensure that it complies with all relevant requirements before a mortgage is made or before advances are made under a construction loan.

compound interest Interest computed on the principal sum *plus* accrued interest.

Comprehensive Environmental Response, Compensation, and Liability Act (CERCLA) A federal law establishing a *Superfund,* to identify parties liable for cleaning operations as well as providing for reimbursement by those parties deemed to be ultimately responsible for cleanup costs.

Comprehensive Loss Underwriting Exchange (CLUE) A database of consumer insurance claims created by ChoicePoint, accessible by nearly 80 percent of insurance companies when they are underwriting or rating an insurance policy.

C

computerized loan origination (CLO) A computer network tied to a major lender that allows agents across the country to initiate mortgage loan applications in their own offices. Such loan origination may be in compliance with RESPA if: (1) full disclosure is made of the fee, (2) multiple lenders are displayed on the computer screen to give the borrower some basis for comparison, and (3) the fee is charged as a dollar amount rather than a percentage of the loan.

concession
 1. A discount given to prospective tenants by landlords to induce them to sign a lease.
 2. A lease of a portion of a premise to conduct a business on property controlled by someone else, such as a refreshment stand at a recreational center.
 3. A franchise right granted by a governmental agency to conduct a business.
 4. In appraising, unusual terms given by a seller that may warrant the buyer paying a higher contract price for a property than would be the case if the seller did not give the special terms.

conciliation agreement A settlement or compromise agreement.

concurrent lease A lease that overlaps the term of an existing shorter-term lease in which the new lessee takes subject to the rights of the first lessee.

concurrent ownership Ownership by two or more persons at the same time, such as joint tenants, tenants by the entirety, tenants in common, or community property owners.

condemnation
1. A judicial or administrative proceeding to exercise the power of eminent domain, that is, the power of the government (federal, state, local, improvement district) to take private property for public use.
2. A decision by the appropriate public agency that a property is no longer fit and must therefore be closed or destroyed.

conditional use zoning A special land use tentatively approved by a zoning ordinance, which ordinarily requires compliance with stated standards.

condo A common reference to a condominium unit or development; refers to either a particular unit or the entire building.

condominium map The detailed site plan of a condo project containing the layout, location, unit numbers, and dimensions of the condominium units, generally filed for record at the same time as the condominium declaration.

condominium owners' association An association of the owners of condominium units to control, regulate, and maintain the common elements in the condominium.

condominium ownership An estate in real property consisting of an individual interest in a unit (residential, commercial, or industrial) and an undivided common interest in the common areas in the condo project such as the land, parking areas, elevators, stairways, exterior structure, and so on.

confession of judgment The act of a debtor in permitting judgment to be entered against him or her by a written statement to that effect without the necessity for the creditor to institute any legal proceedings.

confirmation of sale A court approval of the sale of property by an executor, administrator, guardian, conservator, or commissioner in a foreclosure sale.

conforming loan A standardized conventional loan written on uniform documents that meets the purchase requirements of Fannie Mae and Freddie Mac.

conformity
  1. An appraisal principle of value based on the concept that the more a property or its components are in harmony with the surrounding properties or components, the greater the contributory value.
  2. The concept that maximum value is realized when the four agents of production (labor,

capital, management, and land) are in economic balance.

consequential damages

1. A money award made by a court to compensate an injured party for all losses resulting from a breach of contract, which losses a reasonable person could have foreseen at the time the contract was made.

2. That damage arising from the acts of public bodies or adjacent owners to a given parcel of land that impairs the value of that parcel without actually condemning its use in whole or in part.

conservation A practice by federal, state, and local governments and private landowners of protecting and preserving the natural and scenic resources in order to ensure the highest long-term benefits for all residents.

conservator A guardian, protector, preserver, or receiver appointed by a court to administer the person and property of another (usually an incapable adult) and to ensure that the property will be properly managed.

consideration An act or a promise, which is offered by one party to induce another to enter into a contract; that which is given in exchange for something from another; also the promise to refrain from doing a certain act, like filing a justifiable lawsuit (the forbearance of a right).

consolidate To unite, combine, or incorporate by reference, as in combining two mortgages on one property into a single loan; to combine two or more parcels of land (the reverse of the subdivision process); or to join a land sales registration with an earlier registration.

constant
1. A percentage applied directly to the face value of a debt.
2. The annual payment required per dollar of mortgage money, including both interest and amortized principal.

construction allowance Money or other financial inducement to a lessee that is provided by the lessor to cover the cost, in whole or in part, of preparing a structure for the lessee's occupancy.

construction loan A short-term or interim loan to cover the construction costs of a building or development project, with loan proceeds advanced periodically in the form of installment payments as the work progresses (called *draws*).

constructive An inference created by the law, as in constructive eviction or constructive notice.

constructive eviction Conduct by the landlord that so materially disturbs or impairs a tenant's enjoyment of the leased premises that the tenant is effectively forced to move out and terminate the lease without liability for further rent.

constructive fraud Breach of a legal or equitable duty that the law declares fraudulent because of

C

its tendency to deceive others, despite no showing of dishonesty or intent to deceive.

constructive notice Notice of certain facts that may be discovered by due diligence or inquiry into a public record; a legal presumption that a person is responsible for knowing these facts.

consultant One who gives advice in a specific area, such as a financial adviser.

consumer price index (CPI) A statistical measure of changes in consumer goods prices prepared by the Bureau of Labor Statistics of the Federal Department of Labor.

consummate To bring to completion; the sale of real property is generally consummated upon the closing of the transaction, usually evidenced by delivery of the deed and funds and recording of the conveyance documents.

contiguous In proximity to; adjoining or abutting; near, coterminous (having the same boundaries).

contingency A provision in a contract that requires the completion of a certain act or the happening of a particular event before that contract is binding.

contingency listing A type of listing used in a multiple-listing service that has unusual or special conditions.

continuation An update of a title search, which is "run to date."

continuing education A requirement in most states that real estate and appraiser licensees complete a specified number of educational offerings as a prerequisite to license renewal or reinstatement.

continuous operation clause A shopping center lease provision requiring that key tenants keep their stores in operation during their lease terms.

contour map A topographic map showing the lay of the land of an area by means of a series of lines that connect points of equal elevation at set intervals depending on the scale used.

contract A legally enforceable agreement between competent parties who agree to perform or refrain from performing certain acts for a consideration.

contract documents In terms of real estate development, the agreement between two parties together with all supporting elements that assist in defining, amending, or modifying the agreement and its attendant conditions (drawings, specifications, change orders, addenda).

contract for deed An agreement between the seller (vendor) and buyer (vendee) for the purchase of real property in which the payment of all or a portion of the selling price is deferred.

contract of sale A contract for the purchase and sale of real property in which the buyer agrees to purchase for a certain price and the seller agrees to convey title by way of a deed or an assignment of lease (for leasehold property) binding the parties to the purchase during the period of time required to close the transaction and setting forth the initial directions to the closing agent or escrow company to process the mechanics of the transaction.

contractor One who contracts or covenants, with either a public body or private parties, to construct works or erect buildings at a certain price.

contract price A tax term used in computation of gain realized from an installment sale representing a property's selling price, minus any mortgages assumed or taken subject to by the buyer, plus the excess (if any) of any such liens collected in addition to the seller's adjusted basis at the time of sale, essentially, the seller's equity.

contract rent The rental income as stipulated by the parties in a lease.

contribution An appraisal principle in which the worth of an improvement is what it adds to the entire property's market value, regardless of the actual cost of the improvement.

controlled business arrangements As defined under the Real Estate Settlement Procedures Act (RESPA), an arrangement or combination in which an individual or a firm has more than a 1 percent interest in a company to which the individual or firm regularly refers business.

conventional estate An estate purposely created by the parties to a transaction; differs from an estate created by operation of law, such as a life estate created under dower laws.

C

conventional loan A loan made with real estate as security and not involving government participation in the form of insuring (FHA) or guaranteeing (VA) the loan.

conversion
1. The process of transforming an income-producing property, such as a rental apartment building or hotel, into condominium apartments for sale to separate owners.
2. The appropriation of property belonging to another. The conversion may be illegal (as when a broker misappropriates client funds), or it may be legal (as when the government condemns property under the right of eminent domain).
3. The process of converting from one use to another for tax purposes; for example, changing a personal residence into a rental property.

conveyance The transfer of title or an interest in real property by means of a written instrument such as a deed or an assignment of lease.

co-obligor One sharing in an obligation with another, such as a cosigner of a promissory note.

cooling-off period A kind of grace period provided by law or by contract in which a party to a contract can legally back out of the contract; a right of rescission.

cooperating broker A broker who assists another broker in the sale of real property. Usually, the cooperating broker is the (selling) broker who found the buyer who offers to buy a piece of property that is listed with another (listing) broker.

cooperative ownership Ownership in which shares in the corporation (or partnership or trust) that hold title to the entire apartment building are inseparable from the "proprietary lease."

corporate resolution A summary of a specific action taken by the board of directors of a corporation normally recorded by the corporate secretary in the corporation's minute book.

corporation A legal entity created under state law, consisting of an association of one or more individuals generally including the following characteristics: perpetual existence; centralized management in the board of directors; liability of a shareholder limited to the amount of his or her investment; and free transferability of corporate shares.

corporeal property Tangible real or personal property such as buildings, fixtures, and fences.

correction deed Any type of deed used to correct a prior erroneous deed, as when the grantor's name has been misspelled or when some minor mistake of fact has been made.

correction lines Provisions in the government survey method made to compensate for the curvature of the earth's surface.

corridor development The growth of businesses or plants along major arteries connecting two large industrial or commercial centers some distance from each other.

cosigner An additional person signing a contract or a note and becoming obligated to perform along with the principal party to the contract.

cost approach An approach to the valuation of property consisting of four steps: estimate the land value; estimate the replacement cost of the building new; deduct all accrued depreciation from the replacement cost; and finally add the estimated land value to the depreciated replacement cost.

cost-of-living index An index number indicating the relative change in the cost of living between a selected period of time (using a factor of 100) and another period of time.

cost-plus contract A construction agreement in which the owner pays the cost of all labor and materials plus a certain additional amount based on a set percentage of the cost, representing profit and contractor's overhead.

cotenancy A form of concurrent property ownership in which two or more persons own an undivided interest in the same property.

counseling A specialty within the real estate industry that involves providing skilled, independent advice and professional guidance on a variety of real estate problems.

counteroffer A new offer made in response to an offer received from an offeror that effectively rejects the original offer, which cannot thereafter be accepted unless revived by the offeror's repeating it.

county A governmental division of a state; often large administrative divisions within a state.

court
1. A short roadway partially or wholly enclosed by buildings, giving the impression of a small open square.
2. An open area enclosed on two or more sides by walls or buildings.
3. An official session for the administration of justice—a court of law.

covenant An agreement or promise between two or more parties in which they pledge to perform (or not perform) specified acts on a property; or a written agreement that specifies certain uses or nonuses of the property.

covenant not to compete Agreement given by a seller of a business not to compete against the purchaser in an agreed area for a specified time.

covenants and conditions Covenants are unconditional promises contained in contracts, the breach of which would entitle a person to damages and indicated by words such as *promise, undertake,* and *agree.* Conditions are contingencies, qualifications, or occurrences upon which an estate or property right (like a fee simple) would be gained or lost and are indicated by words such as *if, when, unless,* and *provided.*

covenants, conditions, and restrictions (CC&Rs) Private restrictions on the use of real property; in some states, simply called *restrictions.* Must be enforced by homeowner associations, not municipalities.

covenants running with the land Covenants that become part of the property rights and benefit or bind successive owners of the property.

creative financing A generic term used to describe a wide variety of innovative financing techniques used to market a property.

credit
1. Obligations that are due or are to become due to a person.
2. In closing statements, that which is due and payable to either the buyer or seller—the opposite of a charge or debit.

creditor The person to whom a debtor owes a debt or obligation; a lender.

credit rating A rating given a person or company to establish creditworthiness based on present financial condition, experience, and past credit history.

credit report A report detailing the credit history of a person or business, used to determine credit-worthiness.

credit scoring A financial snapshot of a borrower's credit history and current usage of credit at a given point in time, which affects the availability of, and interest rates for loans.

credit union A cooperative nonprofit organization in which members place money in savings accounts, usually at higher interest rates than at other savings institutions.

cul-de-sac A street that is open at one end only and usually has a circular turnaround at the other end; a blind alley.

curable depreciation Depreciation that can be corrected at a reasonable and economically feasible cost.

curb appeal The impression gained, whether good or bad, of a property when it is first seen, usually from the street while driving by.

curtesy The interest, recognized in some states, of a husband in property owned by his wife at the time of her death.

curvilinear Having boundaries of curved lines used by subdivision developers when designing street and lot layouts, as opposed to the older grid patterns.

cushion An amount of money computed into a contractor's bid for a project to protect the contractor against possible unforeseen occurrences such as delays in governmental approvals, poor weather, and bidding mistakes.

customer The unrepresented third party in an agency relationship.

cyclical movement In economics, shifts in the business cycle of the national economy from prosperity through recession, depression, recovery, and back to prosperity.

D

damages The compensation recoverable in a lawsuit by a complainant who sustained an injury to his or her person or property through the act or default of another.

date Usually the exact day a legal document is signed. Not essential for the validity of most real estate contracts.

datum A level surface to which heights and depths are referred; the datum plane.

days on the market The time period between listing a property and either selling or removing it from the market.

DBA "Doing business as"; used to identify a trade name or a fictitious business name.

dead-end street A street with only one entrance; sometimes leads into a cul-de-sac.

dealer An Internal Revenue Service designation for a person who regularly buys and sells real property in the ordinary course of business.

debenture A type of long-term note or bond given as evidence of debt; unlike a mortgage note, a debenture is not secured by a specific property.

debit A charge on an accounting statement, balance sheet, or closing statement in a real estate transaction; the opposite of a credit.

debt coverage ratio The ratio of annual net income to annual debt service.

D

debt financing The payment, in whole or in part, for a capital investment with borrowed monies, as opposed to investing one's own funds.

debtor One who owes money; a borrower, a maker of a note; a mortgagor.

debt relief The forgiveness of a legal obligation to pay money.

debt service The amount of money needed to meet the periodic payments of principal and interest on a loan or debt that is being amortized.

debt-to-equity ratio The relationship between the total loan owed the lender and the invested capital of the owner; also known as the *leverage ratio*.

decedent A dead person, typically one who has died recently.

declarant The original person or developer creating the condominium, PUD, or townhouse community, who records the appropriate documents, including the CC&Rs.

declaration The legal document that the developer of a condominium must generally file and record in order to create a condominium under state law.

declaration of restrictions A statement of all the covenants, conditions, and restrictions (CC&Rs) that affect a parcel of land. Often noted on the map or plan when recording the subdivision plat, or if numerous, on a separate document called a declaration.

decree A court order or judgment.

D

dedication The transfer of privately owned land to the public without consideration, with the intent that the land will be accepted and used for public purposes.

deductions Ordinary and necessary expenses paid in a taxable year, which reduce the amount of taxable income and therefore tax liability.

deed A written instrument by which a property owner as "grantor" conveys and transfers to a "grantee" an ownership interest in real property. To be valid as between grantor and grantee, a deed must contain the following elements:

> *Grantor:* The deed must name a grantor who is of age and of sound mind.

> *Grantee:* There must be an actual grantee representative.

> *Consideration:* A deed should recite some consideration, although in most instances it need not be the actual consideration.

> *Words of conveyance:* Words of conveyance, such as "I hereby grant and convey" distinguish the deed from a mortgage instrument.

> *Legal description:* There must be a legal description of the land conveyed, such as a metes-and bounds-description; by lot, block, and subdivision; or by a government survey description.

> *Signature:* The grantor must sign the deed.

> *Delivery:* Delivery is the final act of the grantor, and must be delivered and accepted during the lifetime of both the grantor and the grantee to be valid.

Though not essential for validity, a deed is normally recorded to protect the grantee against claims of any third party.

deed in lieu of foreclosure A deed to a lender given by an owner conveying mortgaged property in which the mortgage is in default as an alternative to a foreclosure action.

deed in trust A form of deed by which real estate is conveyed to a trustee, usually to establish a land trust.

deed of reconveyance A document used to transfer legal title from the trustee back to the borrower (trustor) after a debt secured by a deed of trust has been paid to the lender (beneficiary).

deed of trust A legal document in which title to property is transferred to a third-party trustee as security for an obligation owed by the trustor (borrower) to the beneficiary (lender). It is also called a trust deed and is similar to a mortgage.

deed restrictions Provisions placed in deeds to control future uses of the property.

default The nonperformance of a duty or obligation that is part of a contract; in a breach of contract, the nondefaulting party can seek legal remedies to recover any loss.

default judgment A court order in favor of the plaintiff resulting from the defendant's failure to answer a complaint or appear in court to end the action.

defeasance clause A clause used in leases and mortgages to eat or cancel a certain right upon the occurance of a specified condition.

defect of record Any encumbrance on a title that is made a part of the public record.

defendant The person being sued by the plaintiff in a lawsuit; the person charged with the wrong and from whom recovery is sought.

deferred commission A commission that has been earned but not yet fully paid.

deferred maintenance Physical deterioration or loss in value of a building resulting from postponed maintenance to the building.

deferred-payment method An accounting method of reporting taxable income on a deferred basis; also called the **cost-recovery method** or the **return-of-capital method.**

deferred taxes The lawful delay of paying income taxes under specified provisions of the Internal Revenue Code.

deficiency judgment A judgment against a borrower, endorser, or guarantor for the balance of a debt owed when the security for a loan is insufficient to satisfy the debt, as when the foreclosure sale of a property produces less than the amount needed to pay the costs and expenses of the action and to satisfy the obligation secured by the foreclosed mortgage.

delayed exchange An attempt to qualify a real estate transaction as an IRC Section 1031 exchange where "exchange" of the properties is not simultaneous.

delinquent The past-due status of a financial obligation such as a promissory note.

delivery The legal act of transferring ownership; documents such as deeds and mortgages must be delivered and accepted before becoming valid.

demand
1. A letter from a creditor requesting payment of the amount due, as in a loan or lease.
2. The desire for economic goods that can be bought at a certain price, in a given market, at a particular time; what the marketplace will demand.

demand note A promissory note that permits the holder to call in the loan at any time upon notice by the holder.

demise

1. A conveyance of an estate or interest in real property to someone for a certain number of years, for life or at will—most commonly for years, as in a lease.
2. A synonym for *death*.

demography The statistical study of human populations, especially in reference to size, density, and distribution.

density When used in connection with zoning requirements, the number of building units per acre or the number of occupants or families per unit of land area (acre, square mile); usually the ratio of land area to improvement area.

density zoning A type of zoning ordinance generally associated with subdivisions, which restricts the average maximum number of houses per acre that may be built within a particular subdivision.

deposit Money offered by a prospective buyer as an indication of good faith in entering into a contract to purchase; also known as earnest money; security for the buyer's performance of a contract. A deposit is not necessary to create a valid purchase contract because the mutual promises of the parties to buy and to sell are sufficient consideration to enforce the contract.

deposition The formal testimony made by a witness or a party to a lawsuit (the deponent) before the trial.

depreciable life The time period over which cost recovery of an asset is to be allocated. For tax returns, depreciable life may be shorter or longer than estimated service life.

depreciable real property (accounting) A type of property subject to wear and tear and that is used in a trade or business or held for the production of income.

depreciation allowance The accounting charge made to allow for the fact that the asset may become economically obsolete before its physical deterioration.

depreciation (appraisal) In the appraisal cost approach, a loss in value due to any cause; any condition that adversely affects the value of an improvement. Divided into three classes according to its cause: physical deterioration, functional obsolescence, and external obsolescence.

depreciation recapture An Internal Revenue Service provision making excess depreciation taken on real property subject to income tax upon sale of the property.

depreciation (tax) An expense deduction taken for an investment in depreciable property to allow for the recovery of the cost of the investment.

dereliction The gradual receding of water that leaves dry land.

descent The acquisition of an estate by inheritance when an heir succeeds to the property by operation of law; i.e., the ancestor dies intestate.

description The portion of a conveyance document that defines the property being transferred.

designated agent In some states, where allowed by law, a designated agent is the agent for either the buyer or the seller to the exclusion of all other agents in the brokerage; another salesperson in the firm could be designated the agent of the other party without thereby creating a dual agency for the individual agents.

developer One who attempts to put land to its most profitable use through the construction of improvements, such as commercial condominiums or subdivision projects.

development impact fee An amount of money charged a developer by a local governmental body to cover the costs of providing essential services to the proposed project, such as fire and police protection and road maintenance.

development loan A loan to cover the costs of improving property; an interim loan.

development rights The rights a landowner sells to another to develop and improve the property.

devise A transfer of real property under a will. The donor is the *devisor,* and the recipient is the *devisee.*

diluvion The gradual and imperceptible washing away and resultant loss of soil along a watercourse; opposite of *alluvion.*

direct endorsement Ability of an FHA-approved lender to secure FHA single- and multi-family mortgage insurance by following FHA guidelines, reducing delays and red tape sometimes associated with FHA-insured loans.

direct reduction mortgage   A mortgage that requires payment of a fixed amount of principal each period (loan recapture); total payments vary, as the interest portion is reduced with each payment.

direct sales comparison approach A method of appraising or valuing real property based on the principle of substitution (comparison), most frequently used in appraising residential property.

disability   See the legal term **handicap**.

disbursement   Money paid out, or expended, in an accounting process such as an escrow closing.

discharge of contract Cancellation or termination of a contract, such as mutual cancellation; rescission;   performance   or   nonperformance; accord and satisfaction; illegality; and in certain circumstances, to the extent a court will not enforce the contract, by the statute of limitations, the statute of frauds, and the Bankruptcy Act.

disclaimer A statement denying legal responsibility, frequently found in the form of the statement, "There are no promises, representations, oral understandings, or agreements except as contained herein" but does not relieve the maker of any liabilities for fraudulent acts or misrepresentations.

disclosure   To reveal, make known.

disclosure statement
1. An information report required under the federal Truth-in-Lending Act to be given to consumer borrowers by creditors.
2. Any statement of fact required by law, such as the settlement disclosure required under the federal Real Estate Settlement Procedures Act or the federal lead-based paint disclosures for property built before 1978.
3. Information conveyed by the seller of the property to the buyer, and now required by many states in the transfer of one-to-four dwelling properties.

discount To sell at a reduced value; the difference between face value and cash value.

discount broker A licensed real estate broker who specifically provides brokerage services at lower rates than most brokers do.

discounted cash flow Used in measuring return from a real estate investment, the present value of a future income stream as determined by a given discount rate (using present value tables).

discounting The appraisal process of mathematically computing the value of a property based on the present worth of anticipated future cash flows or income.

discount points An added loan fee charged by a lender to increase the yield on a lower-than-market-interest loan and to make the loan more competitive with higher-interest loans.

discount rate
1. An annual competitive rate of return on total invested capital necessary to compensate the investor for the risks inherent in a particular investment.
2. The rate at which the Federal Reserve lends money to its eligible banks.

D

discovery The legal process by which lawyers preparing for trial can require witnesses for the other side to produce documents and answer written or oral questions.

discretionary funds Money available for investment; money in excess of that needed for basic needs.

discrimination The act of making a distinction against or in favor of a person on the basis of the group or class to which the person belongs; the failure to treat people equally under the law.

disparate impact A legal doctrine used in federal discrimination cases to show a violation even when the defendant's actions have no apparent relationship to a protected class. In a disparate impact case, intent to discriminate is not necessary.

disposal field A drainage area, not close to the water supply, where waste from a septic tank disperses.

dispossess proceedings Legal action to evict someone not in legal possession.

distraint A common-law concept that allows a landlord to seize a tenant's belongings for rents in arrears; most states now require a court order.

distressed property Property that brings an insufficient return to the owner or is in difficulty for other reasons.

divided interest An interest in various parts of a whole property, such as the interest of the fee owner, lessee, or mortgagee.

D

documents Legal instruments such as conveyancing documents (deeds, leases, and mortgages), contracts (options, exchange, and purchase agreements), and other legal forms (wills and bills of sale).

domicile From *domus,* Latin for "house." The state where an individual has his or her true, fixed permanent home and principal business establishment and where that person has the intention of returning whenever he or she is absent from it.

dominant estate (tenement) The estate that attaches to and derives benefit from the servient estate in reference to an easement appurtenant.

Do Not Call Registry A national registry maintained by the Federal Trade Commission (FTC) of telephone numbers whose owners do not wish to receive telemarketing calls.

donor One who gives or makes a gift to the recipient, the donee.

double entry In reference to a settlement or closing statement, the practice of entering a dollar amount as both a debit entry and a credit entry; on a closing statement, taxes paid in arrears would be prorated and appear as a credit to the buyer and a debit to the seller.

double escrow Two concurrent escrows on the same property, in which the seller attempts to use the buyer's money to acquire title to property X in one escrow to be able to convey title to property X to the buyer in the second escrow.

double taxation Two or more taxes paid for the same asset or financial transaction, and is often used in reference to income taxes assessed first on the corporate level and secondly as dividend income on the earnings distributed to the shareholders.

dower The legal right or interest recognized in some states that a wife acquires in the property her husband held or acquired any time during their marriage, an interest that does not actually become a legal estate (called *consummate dower*) until the husband's death.

down payment The amount of cash a purchaser pays at the time of purchase.

downzoning A change in zoning from a higher to a lower classification or from a more active to less active classification, such as from residential to conservation use, or multifamily to single-family use.

drainage A system of gradually drawing off water and moisture from land, naturally or artificially, by means of pipes and conduits.

draw An advancement of money to be applied against either commissions earned but not paid or future commissions. Also, the periodic advancing of funds under a construction loan agreement.

Drug Enforcement Act A 1988 federal law establishing the right of federal drug enforcement authorities to seize real property on which illegal drug activity is taking place.

dry closing A closing that is complete except for the final act of disbursing funds and delivering documents.

dry mortgage A mortgage or deed of trust in which the lender looks solely to the real property for recovery of the debt in case of default; that is, there is no personal liability for any deficiency upon foreclosure; a nonrecourse mortgage.

dual agency (limited agency) A situation in which an agent (or agency in some states) represents both principals to a transaction and is illegal in some states. States that allow dual agency generally require that licensees gain consent to the "potential" of dual agency early in the relationship and written consent by both parties is generally required before an offer is written and submitted.

dual contract An improper or fraudulent contract to buy property that contains terms and financial conditions that differ from the original or true agreement and falsely represents the parties' true intentions. A broker who participates in any way in the preparation of a dual contract may be subject to license suspension or revocation, a fine for misconduct, or civil damages.

due date A date set in a note or contract for payment to be made.

due diligence
1. A fair, proper, and due degree of care and activity.
2. A term used in securities law to refer to the duty of the issuer or broker to ensure that the offering prospectus is accurate and does not misstate or omit material information.
3. A time period in which a buyer is given the opportunity to have experts inspect the property, examine the title, and review the leases to determine whether the property matches the buyer's needs.

due-on-sale clause An acceleration clause found in most mortgage loans, requiring the mortgagor to pay off the mortgage debt when the property is sold, resulting in automatic maturity of the note at the lender's option, effectively eliminating the possibility of the new buyer's assuming the mortgage unless the mortgagee permits the assumption.

duplex A two-family dwelling that provides housing accommodations for two families and supplies each with separate entrances, kitchens, bedrooms, living rooms, and bathrooms.

durable power of attorney A power of attorney instrument containing language to the effect the power of the attorney in fact will continue beyond the physical or mental incapacity of the principal but terminating upon death of the principal.

duress Unlawful force or action by one person against another in an attempt to coerce the person to perform some act against his or her will; the threat of force is called *menace*.

dwelling Any building, structure, or part thereof used and occupied for human habitation or intended to be so used, including any appurtenances.

dwelling unit As defined in many zoning codes, a room (or connected rooms) constituting an independent housekeeping unit for a family and containing a single kitchen, unlike a hotel room.

E

early occupancy Refers to the practice of allowing the buyer to take possession of real property before closing.

earnest money The cash deposit (including initial and additional deposits) paid by the prospective buyer of real property as evidence of good-faith intention to complete the transaction; called *bargain money, caution money, hand money,* or a *binder* in some states; negotiable between the parties, and serves as a source of payment of damages should the buyer default.

easement A nonpossessory (incorporeal) property interest that one person (the benefited party) has in land owned by another (the burdened party), entitling the holder of the interest to limited use or enjoyment of the other's land; may be terminated by merger, abandonment, release, purpose, operation of law, and overburdening.

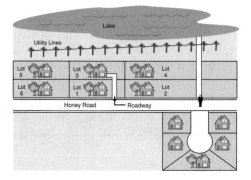

easement appurtenant An easement that runs with the land, binding on subsequent owners.

easement by necessity An easement created by a court of law in cases where justice and necessity dictate it, especially in a classic landlocked situation, requiring two essential elements: must have been a common grantor of the dominant and servient estates, and reasonable necessity for the easement, not merely convenience.

easement by prescription A right acquired by an adverse user to use the land of another; the use must be adverse, hostile, open, notorious, and continuous for the statutory period.

easement in gross The limited right of one person to use another's land (servient estate) when such right is *not* created for the benefit of any land owned by the owner of the easement, i.e., there is no dominant estate, because the easement attaches personally to the owner, not to the land.

economic life The estimated period over which an improved property may be profitably utilized so that it yields a return over and above the economic rent attributable to the land itself; the period during which an improvement has value in excess of its salvage value.

economic obsolescence A specific kind of external obsolescence in which a reduction in value is caused by a situation that adversely affects the economics of an area, such as the relocation of a major industry.

economic rent The rental income (market rent) that real estate can command in an open, competitive market at any given time, as contrasted with contract rent, or the income actually received under a lease agreement.

effective age The apparent age of a building (improvement) based on observed condition rather than chronological age.

effective gross income The anticipated income resulting from the estimated potential gross income from a rental property less an allowance for vacancy and bad debts.

effective interest rate The actual rate or yield of a loan, regardless of the amount stated on the debt instrument.

effective rate
1. The average lease rate of a property per square foot after deducting negotiated concessions.
2. A payment amount on certain mortgage notes—usually buydown types—that offer lower payment amounts that are calculated with an "effective rate" that is less than the face rate.

effective yield A calculation of the return on investment that considers the price paid, the time held, and the interest charged.

efficiency unit or apartment A small, compact apartment unit; a combination living room/bedroom, kitchenette, and bathroom.

egress A way to exit from a property; the opposite of ingress.

ejectment A legal action by an owner to regain possession of real property from someone who is not legally in possession of real property, such as a trespasser (potential adverse possessor) or a tenant at sufferance whose lease has expired, or in an action by a mortgagee to get possession from a defaulting mortgagor.

elderly housing Housing occupied by persons age 62 or older.

election of remedies Selection from several alternative courses of action to remedy a breach of contract.

elective share A minimum share of a deceased spouse's probate estate, which a surviving spouse may claim in lieu of any amount specified in the deceased spouse's will; usually found in states that have abolished dower and curtesy.

electromagnetic fields (EMFs) Energy fields, naturally occurring, or created found near power lines.

elevation sheet Drawings providing views of the front and sides of a building as it will appear when completed.

emblement A growing crop (called *fructus industriales*), such as corn, which is produced annually through labor and industry; regarded as personal property even before harvest, owned by the tenant who planted the crop.

eminent domain The right of government to take private property for a necessary public use, with just compensation paid to the owner; if the parties cannot agree, the legal action is called *condemnation*.

employee One who works under the supervision and control of another.

empty nesters An older family whose children have grown and left home.

E

enabling legislation A statute creating the power or authority to carry out an activity, as under the provisions of a federal housing program, or to do something not previously authorized.

encroachment An unauthorized invasion or intrusion of an improvement or other real property onto another's property, thus reducing the size and value of the invaded property.

encumbrance Any claim, lien, charge, or liability attached to and binding on real property that may lessen its value or burden, obstruct, or impair the use of a property but not necessarily prevent transfer of title; a right or interest in a property held by one who is not the legal owner of the property.

Endangered Species Act A federal law originally intended to protect endangered species on federal lands but since expanded to control land use for the protection of certain fish, animal, and plant life.

end loan A permanent mortgage used to finance the purchase of a new condominium unit or a lot within a developed subdivision; often called *takeout financing*.

endorsement
1. A method of transferring title to a negotiable instrument, such as a check or promissory note, by signing the owner's name on the reverse side of such instrument.
2. A notation added to an instrument after its execution to change or clarify the document's contents.

enrolled agent A tax professional licensed by the federal government to deal with the Internal Revenue Service on behalf of consumers.

enterprise zone An area in which firms locate their businesses to receive tax breaks and government regulatory benefits.

entitlement
  1. To be owed something under the law.
  2. That portion of a VA-guaranteed loan that protects a lender if the veteran defaults.

E

entity (legal) Any person or artificial being such as a corporation, partnership, proprietorship, or association that has the legal capacity to enter into contractual arrangements that can result in debts and other obligations, and which can sue and be sued.

entrepreneur One who takes the initiative to organize, start, and manage an enterprise or business, usually assuming a substantial portion of the risks, losses, and profits; a promoter or developer.

environmental audit An independent inspection of real property to evaluate compliance with applicable federal, state, and local regulations, systems, programs, and policies for all lands, facilities, and operations supervised by the Department of the Interior.

environmental impact statement (EIS) A report required by the National Environmental Policy Act (NEPA) of all federal agencies that propose projects that can significantly affect the environment locally and regionally.

Environmental Protection Agency (EPA) A federal agency created in 1970 to protect human health and the environment.

environmental regulations Standards set by the federal EPA and state departments of health to control air, water, noise pollution, and other environmental conditions, including the cleanup of hazardous substances.

environmental risk The risk associated with the ownership of real property involving environmental hazards such as contaminated building materials and pollutants, as well as nonhazardous conditions such as wetlands and endangered species.

environmental site assessment (ESA) An investigation by an environmental engineer or other well-qualified specialist to determine if there are any environmental hazards or concerns that affect the use of a property or impose future financial liability.

Equal Credit Opportunity Act (ECOA) Federal legislation passed in 1974 to extend credit based on the applicant's ability to repay the loan and without regard to the applicant's race, color, religion, national origin, sex, marital status, age, or receipt of income from public assistance programs (food stamps, Social Security), and ensure good-faith exercise of any right under the Consumer Credit Protection Act.

equalization board A state or county reviewing agency with the power to adjust certain inequities in tax assessments.

equitable conversion A rule of law created to give the buyer title to the property under an executory contract of sale for certain purposes before the date set for closing, i.e., that immediately upon the making of the contract, the seller holds the legal title for the buyer, who has the beneficial, equitable title.

E

equitable lien A lien arising out of a written contract that shows an intention of the parties to charge some particular property as security for a debt or obligation.

equitable servitude An easement of use enforced in equity that permits restrictive covenants not running with the land to be enforced as though they do run with the land.

equitable title The transferable interest held by a vendee under a purchase contract, contract for deed, or an installment purchase agreement; the equitable right to obtain absolute ownership to property when legal title is in another's name.

equity That interest or value remaining in property after payment of all liens or other charges on the property.

equity build-up The gradual reduction of outstanding principal due on the mortgage, usually through periodic amortized payments.

equity mortgage A line of credit made against the equity in the borrower's home, based on a percentage of the appraised value of the home, minus any outstanding mortgage.

equity of redemption The right of a mortgagor, *before* a foreclosure sale, to reclaim property forfeited due to mortgage default; any right to redeem *after* a foreclosure sale must be created by state statute.

E

equity participation The arrangement between a potential buyer and an investor in which the investor shares an equity interest in a real property purchase in exchange for assisting with the financing of the acquisition.

equity sharing loan A loan in which a resident-owner splits his or her equity or the increase in the value of the home with an investor-owner, who contributes toward the down payment and also to monthly payments and benefits in deducting a share of the tax write-offs.

erosion The gradual loss of soil due to the operation of currents, tides, or winds; the opposite of accretion.

errors and omissions (E&O) insurance A form of insurance that covers liabilities for errors, mistakes, and negligence in the usual listing and selling activities of a real estate office or escrow company, but does not cover fraudulent behavior or punitive damages or claims based on transactions for the personal account of a real estate agent.

escalator clause A contract provision permitting an adjustment of certain payments, not controlled by either party, to move up or down to cover certain contingencies.

escape clause
1. A contract provision relieving a party of liability for failure to perform, as where a stated contingency does not occur.
2. A clause in a proprietary lease of a tenant-stockholder that permits the tenant to surrender the stock and lease back to the cooperative association and thereby terminate continuing liability for payments due under the lease.

escheat The reversion of property to the state or county, as provided by state law, in cases where a decedent dies intestate and there are no heirs capable of inheriting or when the property is abandoned.

escrow The process, in some parts of the country, by which a disinterested third person (a stakeholder) holds money and/or documents until satisfaction of the terms and conditions of the escrow instructions has been achieved, after which delivery and transfer of the escrowed funds and documents takes place. (Escrow should not be confused with closings.)

escrow instructions In a sales transaction, a written statement signed by buyer and seller, which details the procedures necessary to close a transaction and directs the escrow agent how to proceed.

estate

1. The degree, quantity, nature, and extent of ownership interest that a person has in real property, referring to one's legal interest or rights, not to the physical quantity of land.

2. The property owned by a decedent that may be subject to probate administration, federal and state tax, and claims by creditors.

E

estate of inheritance A freehold estate passed by descent or by will after the owner's death, such as a fee simple absolute, not a life estate.

estate tax, federal An excise tax imposed under the Internal Revenue Code by the federal government upon the transfer of property from the estate of a deceased to a beneficiary upon, or by reason of, the decedent's death.

estoppel A legal doctrine by which a person is prevented from asserting rights or facts that are inconsistent with a previous position or representation made by act, conduct, or silence.

et al. Latin abbreviation for *et alii,* meaning "and others."

ethics A system of moral principles, rules, and standards of conduct.

ethnic group A group of people identified by a common heritage of language, culture, customs, race, religion, national origin, language, kinship, and/or cultural similarities.

et ux. Latin abbreviation for *et uxor,* meaning "and wife."

et vir. Latin for "and husband."

eviction

1. The legal process of removing a tenant from the premises for some breach of the lease.

2. The disturbance of a tenant's enjoyment of all or any material part of the leased premises by act of the landlord or by claim of a superior title by a third party.

evidence of title Proof of ownership of property such as a certificate of title, title insurance policy or, with Torrens-registered property, a Torrens certificate of title.

E

examination, licensing Prior to obtaining a real estate license, a written examination required in all states of an applicant who must demonstrate a reasonable knowledge of general real property laws and principles, documents, and state licensing laws.

exception

1. As used in a conveyance of real property, the exclusion from the conveyance of some part of the property granted.

2. Liens and encumbrances specifically excluded from coverage under a title insurance policy.

3. Those matters noted in the "subject to" clause of the contract of sale, in which the seller agrees to convey clear and marketable title "subject to the following exceptions."

excess condemnation The taking of more land than is actually used to meet the public purpose of the condemnation.

exchange A transaction in which all or part of the consideration for the purchase of real property is the transfer of property of "like kind" (i.e., real estate for real estate) to defer the capital gains tax until the property is later disposed of in a taxable transaction; often called a "1031."

E

excise tax A direct tax, imposed without assessment, and measured according to the amount of services performed, income received, or similar criteria; examples include license fees, sales tax, and federal estate tax.

exclusionary zoning The zoning of an area in such a way as to exclude minorities and low-income people.

exclusive agency A written listing agreement giving a sole agent the right to sell a property for a specified time, but the owner reserves the right to sell the property without owing a commission.

exclusive listing A written listing of real property in which the seller agrees to appoint, and compensate, only one broker to sell the property for a specified period of time.

exclusive right to sell A written listing agreement appointing a broker the exclusive agent for the sale of property for a specified period of time entitling the broker to a commission if the property is sold by the owner, the broker, or anyone else.

exculpatory clause
1. A clause inserted in a mortgage note in which the lender waives the right to a deficiency judgment.
2. As used in a lease, a clause that intends to clear or relieve the landlord from liability for tenants' personal injury and property damage.

execute The act of making a document legally valid, such as formalizing a contract by signing, or acknowledging and delivering a deed.

executed contract A fully performed contract.

execution A judicial process whereby the court directs an officer to levy (seize) the property of a judgment debtor in satisfaction of a judgment lien.

executor A person appointed by a testator to carry out the directions and requests in his or her last will and testament, and to dispose of his or her property according to the provisions of the will.

executory contract A contract in which one or both parties has not yet performed, such as a contract for sale.

exhibit A document or section of a document presented as part of the supporting data for the principal document.

expansion option A provision in a lease granting a tenant the option to lease additional adjacent space after a specified period of time.

expert witness A person qualified to render testimony by virtue of specialized knowledge and/or experience.

exposure
1. Where and/or how a property is situated in terms of compass direction or its accessibility to air, light, or facilities.
2. In marketing terms, a property for sale given visibility in the open market.

expropriation The taking of private land for a public purpose under the government's right of eminent domain, as exercised in a condemnation suit.

extended coverage
1. A term used widely in fire insurance policies to denote that the policies cover damage by wind, hail, explosion, riot, smoke, and other perils.
2. A title insurance policy that covers risks normally excluded by most standard-coverage policies.

extender clause A "carryover" clause (often referred to as a *safety clause* or *protection clause*) in a listing that provides that a broker is still entitled to a commission for a set period of time after the listing has expired if the property is sold to a prospect of the broker introduced to the property during the period of the listing.

extension An agreement to continue the period of performance beyond a specified period.

exterior insulating and finish system (EIFS) A multilayered exterior siding system used on commercial buildings and homes, also called synthetic stucco.

external obsolescence A loss of value (typically incurable) resulting from extraneous factors that exist outside of property itself; a type of depreciation caused by environmental, social, or economic forces over which an owner has little or no control.

F

face value
1. The amount due at the maturity of an instrument; the par value as shown on its face, not the real or market value.
2. The dollar amount of insurance coverage.

facilitator A real estate licensee who assists a buyer and seller in reaching agreement in a real estate transaction but does not have an agency relationship with that party.

factory built construction Anyconstruction product that is built all or in part in the controlled conditions of a factory.

Fair Credit Reporting Act (FCRA) A federal law designed to protect the public from the reporting of inaccurate information by credit agencies, including ChoicePoint, an agency that gathers information for the insurance industry.

Fair Debt Collection Practices Act A federal law regulating the activities of debt collectors when collecting consumer debts; providing protection from illegal and unethical debt collection tactics, including specific rules on how collectors can communicate with consumers at home and at work. Prescribes the types and timing of notices required prior to collecting the debts.

Fair Housing Amendment Act of 1988 An amendment to the federal Fair Housing Act that added two more protected classes: those physically and mentally handicapped and those with children under 18 years of age ("familial status").

fair market value (FMV) An appraisal term for the most probable price in terms of money that a property, if offered for sale for a reasonable period of time in a competitive market, would bring to a seller who is willing but not compelled to sell, from a buyer who is willing but not compelled to buy, both parties being fully informed of all the purposes to which the property is best adapted and ways it is capable of being used.

false advertising Advertising that contains blatantly false or misleading information.

familial status As defined in the Fair Housing Act, a protected class consisting of one or more individuals under age 18 living with a parent or legal guardian or another person given written permission from a parent; also protected are pregnant women, a person in the process of securing legal custody, and foster parents.

F

family In the traditional sense, persons related to each other by blood or marriage and today, may include a broader interpretation to include certain nontraditional living arrangements.

Fannie Mae A private, shareholder-owned company that does not lend money directly to home-buyers, but works in the secondary market, buying mortgage loans to ensure that mortgage money is readily available.

farm area A real estate licensee's term to indicate either a selected geographical area or a group of people from which to solicit real estate business and to which a real estate salesperson devotes special attention and study.

F

farm assets The component assets of a ranch or farm, including farmland; personal residence; other residences and structures used in the business of farming or ranching; vines, trees, pipelines, fences, irrigation systems, livestock; and unharvested crops sold to the purchaser and subject to special treatment for income-tax purposes, as provided for in the Internal Revenue Code.

Farm Credit System A federal program designed to serve the unique financial requirements of farmers, ranchers, producers, and harvesters of agricultural products, rural homeowners, and owners of selected farm-related businesses.

Farmer Mac The nickname of the Federal Agricultural Mortgage Corporation.

Farmer's Home Administration (FmHA)   Formerly, a federal agency under the U.S. Department of Agriculture, now replaced by the Rural Housing Service (RHS).

farmland   Land used specifically for agricultural purposes in the raising of crops or livestock. Also land designated in zoning laws for agricultural purposes.

fastrack construction   A construction method in which building commences under a negotiated contract before all plans and specifications have been completed.

feasibility study
1. An analysis of a proposed subject or property with emphasis on the attainable income, probable expenses, and most advantageous use and design.
2. A survey of an urban area using federal funds to determine whether it is practicable to undertake an urban renewal project within that area.

Federal Agricultural Mortgage Corporation (FAMC)   A federal agency that operates as a separate entity within the Farm Credit System to develop a secondary market in farm real estate loans, known as Freddie Mac.

Federal Deposit Insurance Corporation (FDIC)   An arm of the U.S. Treasury Department responsible for administering bank depository insurance in the United States and insuring cash deposits, including certificates of deposits up to $100,000 each, which have been placed in member institutions.

Federal Emergency Management Agency (FEMA) A federal agency now part of the U.S. Department of Homeland Security (DHS) responsible for disaster mitigation, preparedness, response, and recovery planning, and managing the National Flood Insurance Program and the U.S. Fire Administration.

federal fair housing law A federal law enacted in 1968 and subsequently amended, Title VIII of the Civil Rights Act is called the *Federal Fair Housing Act*. This act declared a national policy of providing housing throughout the United States without regard to race, color, sex, familial status, handicap, religion, or national origin in connection with the sale or rental of most dwellings (including time-sharing units) and any vacant land offered for residential construction or use. There are only a few exceptions to the law. Two remedial avenues, one administrative and one judicial, are available. The burden of proof is on the complainant.

Federal Financial Institutions Examinations Council (FFIEC) A council of federal regulatory agency representatives organized to promote uniformity among commercial banks, savings associations, and credit unions.

Federal Home Loan Banks A class of federally chartered savings associations and 12 regional Federal Home Loan Banks that provides a credit reserve for its members; established in 1932.

Federal Housing Administration (FHA) A federal agency established to encourage improvement in housing standards and conditions, to provide an adequate home-financing system through the insurance of housing mortgages and credit, and to exert a stabilizing influence on the mortgage market. FHA is part of HUD and neither builds homes nor lends money directly, but instead insures loans on real property, including condominiums, made by approved lending institutions. FHA loans are limited to loan amounts that vary regionally.

federal land bank (FLB) A privately owned cooperative organization administered by the Farm Credit Administration to provide low-cost, long-term loans to farmers and livestock corporations that belong to the Federal Land Bank Association.

federally related transactions Any sale transaction that ultimately involves a federal agency in either the primary or secondary mortgage market.

Federal National Mortgage Association (FNMA) The original name of Fannie Mae.

Federal Reserve System ("the Fed") The nation's central bank created by the Federal Reserve Act of 1913 to help stabilize the economy through the judicious handling of the money supply and credit available in this country, functioning through a seven-member Board of Governors and 12 Federal Reserve District Banks, by setting policies and working with privately owned commercial banks.

federal revenue stamp A documentary transfer tax, abolished in 1968, levied by the federal government upon the transfer of title to real property. Payment was evidenced by red stamps placed on the document.

federal savings and loan association A savings and loan institution that is federally chartered and privately owned by shareholders (stock savings and loan) or depositors (mutual savings and loan) under the regulatory authority of the Office of Thrift Supervision; its deposits are insured by the Savings Association Insurance Fund (SAIF).

federal tax lien A lien that attaches to real property if either the federal estate tax is not paid or the taxpayer has violated the federal income tax or payroll tax laws.

Federal Trade Commission (FTC) A federal agency created to investigate and eliminate unfair and deceptive trade practices or unfair methods of competition in interstate commerce, enforcing the federal Truth-in-Lending laws, and monitoring compliance of the Equal Credit Opportunity Act, the Fair Credit Reporting Act, and the Home Mortgage Disclosure Act.

federal underwriters Four federal agencies—Fannie Mae, Ginnie Mae, Freddie Mac, and FAMC—authorized to issue guarantees as credit enhancement for mortgage-backed securities.

fee appraiser A professional who furnishes appraisal services for a fee, rendering an appraisal of a parcel of real property and typically submitting an appraisal report.

fees for service An alternative to traditional brokerage fees in which real estate service charges are "unbundled" and the consumer only pays for services actually used.

fee simple The maximum possible estate one can possess in real property, of indefinite duration, freely transferable, and inheritable.

fee simple defeasible An estate in land in which the holder has a fee simple title subject to being divested upon the happening of a specified condition; also called a qualified fee or a defeasible fee.

felony A serious crime punishable by imprisonment in a state or federal prison.

feudal system An ancient system of land ownership under which the government or king held title to all lands and the individual was merely a tenant whose rights of use and occupancy of real property were held at the sufferance of an overlord.

FICO Score Mathematical scores developed by the Fair Isaac Company and used by credit bureaus and lenders to evaluate the risk associated in lending money; scores range from 450 to 850; the lower the score, the higher the risk.

fictitious company name A business name other than that of the person under whom the business is registered, for example "XYZ Real Estate" or "Greenfields Realty."

fidelity bond Also known as a *surety bond,* a fidelity bond purchased by an employer to cover his or her employees who are entrusted with sums of money or are responsible for valuable assets.

fiduciary A relationship that implies a position of trust and confidence wherein one person is usually entrusted to hold or manage property or money for another.

file To place an original document on public record.

F

filled land An area where the grade has been raised by depositing or dumping dirt, gravel, or rock.

finance charge The total of all costs imposed directly or indirectly by the creditor and payable directly or indirectly by the customer, as defined by the federal Truth-in-Lending Act.

finance fee DEA mortgage brokerage fee to cover the expenses incurred in placing a mortgage with a lending institution; a mortgage service charge or origination fee.

financial institution An intermediary organization that obtains funds through deposits and then lends those funds to earn a return.

Financial Institutions Reform, Recovery, and Enforcement Act (FIRREA) A comprehensive law passed in 1989 to provide guidelines for the regulation of financial institutions; created the Savings Association Insurance Fund (SAIF) and the Bank Insurance Fund (BIF). Restructured the Federal Deposit Insurance Corporation (FDIC), created the Appraisal Foundation, and requires the use of state-certified or state-licensed appraisers to appraise properties involving a federally insured or federally regulated industry.

financial statement A formal statement of the financial status and net worth of a person or company, setting forth and classifying assets and liabilities as of a specified date.

financing That part of the purchase price for a property exclusive of the down payment, consisting of financing instruments such as mortgages, deeds of trust, contracts for deed, and the like.

financing statement A brief document (required under the Uniform Commercial Code) filed to "perfect" or establish a creditor's security interest in a chattel or other personal property. In real estate this protects the creditor's interest in personal property that is used as security for a debt, but that becomes a fixture when it is attached to realty.

finder's fee A fee paid to someone for producing either a buyer to purchase or a seller to list property; also called a referral fee.

fire insurance A form of property insurance covering losses due to fire, usually not as comprehensive as a homeowner's insurance policy that includes coverage against other perils, including liability.

fire sprinkler system A fire protection system activated by heat within a given building area, which automatically provides a flow of pressurized water from overhead nozzles when the temperature exceeds a certain predetermined level.

firm commitment A definite undertaking by a lender to lend a set amount of money at a specified interest rate for a certain term; also, a commitment by the FHA to insure a mortgage on certain property to a specified mortgagor.

first mortgage A mortgage on property that is superior in right to any other mortgage; absent subordination, it must be recorded first.

first-year depreciation Under IRS Code Section 179, a provision that allows a sole proprietor, partnership, or corporation to fully expense tangible property in the year in which it is purchased.

fiscal year A business year used for tax, corporate, or accounting purposes, as opposed to a calendar year.

five-year forecast A long-term projection of estimated income and expense for a property based on predictable changes.

fixed expenses Those recurring expenses that have to be paid regardless of whether the property is occupied, for example, real property taxes, hazard insurance, and debt service.

fixed-rate loan A loan with the same rate of interest for the life of the loan.

fixer-upper A property needing a lot of repair work, usually sold below market value.

fixing-up expenses Expenses (such as painting and carpet cleaning) incurred in repairing and refurbishing a primary residence in order to facilitate its sale.

fixture

1. An article (such as a stove, a bookcase, plumbing, track lighting, or tile) that was once personal property but has been so affixed to real estate that it has become real property.
2. Trade or tenant fixtures installed by the tenant remain personal property and normally can be removed by a business tenant at the termination of the lease.
3. The permanent parts of a plumbing system, such as toilets and bathtubs.

flag lot A land parcel having the configuration of an extended flag and pole that permits access to the site, which is usually located to the rear of another lot fronting a main street.

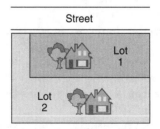

flexible payment mortgage A loan that employs a computerized method of calculating the payments required by a pledged account mortgage.

flip A transaction in which one party contracts to buy a property with the intention to transfer quickly (flip) the property over to the ultimate buyer.

FLIP® Flexible loan insurance payment mortgage.

float
1. A mortgage banking term that refers to the spread of the variable interest rate on a loan; the "pegged rate."
2. A banking term that refers to a check that has not yet been cleared for collection.

F

flood insurance Insurance offered by private companies backed by the federal government, designed to provide coverage for damage from floods, tidal waves, or any rising water. Flood insurance is always a separate policy, never part of a homeowner's policy.

The HUD-1 requires a Flood Certification and if the certification indicates that the property is located in a Special Flood Hazard Area (SFHA) (Zones A, V, or AV), then federal banking laws mandate flood insurance. Lenders have options whether or not to require flood insurance for properties not located in a SFHA.

Flood Insurance Rate Map Official maps showing areas within the 100-year-flood boundary, which are designated *Special Flood Hazard Areas* and further divided into insurance risk zones.

floodplain The flat portions of land located along watercourses and streams, which are subject to overflow and flooding.

F

floor area ratio The ratio of floor area to land area (often land on which the building sits), expressed as a percent or decimal and is determined by dividing the total floor area of the building by the lot area.

floor duty The frequent practice in real estate brokerage offices of assigning one sales agent the responsibility for handling all telephone calls and office visitors for a specified period of time and allowing the "floor person" to meet prospects if the caller does not ask to speak to a particular salesperson.

floor plan The architectural drawings showing the floor layout of a building, including the exact room sizes and their interrelationships.

foot-candle A determination of light intensity.

footing A concrete support under a foundation, chimney, or column that usually rests on solid ground and is wider than the structure being supported.

forbearance The act of refraining from taking legal action despite the fact that payment of a promissory note in a mortgage or deed of trust is in arrears.

force and effect of law A phrase referring to the fact that an administrative regulation has the same legal significance as a legislative act.

forced sale An involuntary sale resulting from the owner's failure to make payments to outstanding creditors.

forecast Estimate of the outcome of future occurrences, particularly financial statements of future periods based on such estimates.

foreclosure A legal procedure whereby property used as security for a debt is sold to satisfy the debt in the event of default in payment of the mortgage note or default of other terms in the mortgage document. A judicial foreclosure provides that, upon sufficient public notice, the property may be sold by court order. A *nonjudicial foreclosure* permits the lender (or the lender's trustee if a deed of trust is used) the right to sell the mortgaged property upon default without being required to spend the time and money involved in a court foreclosure suit.

F

foreign corporation Any corporation organized under the laws of another state or country and not organized under a given state's laws but that conducts a portion of its business in that state.

Foreign Investment in Real Property Tax Act (FIRPTA) A federal law designed to subject non-resident aliens and foreign corporations to U.S. income tax upon their gain from the disposition of a U.S. real property interest.

forfeiture Loss of the right to something as a result of nonperformance of an obligation or condition.

forgery The illegal act of counterfeiting documents or making a false signature, alteration, or falsification.

formaldehyde A colorless organic compound with a strong pronounced odor that can be readily identified and measured, classified by the EPA as a "probable human carcinogen."

for sale by owner (FSBO) A situation in which the owner attempts to sell a property without listing it with a real estate broker; pronounced "fizzbo."

foundation wall The masonry or concrete walls below ground level that serve as the main support for the frame structure.

fractional interest A partial interest in real estate representing less than the full bundle of rights, e.g., a subleasehold interest.

franchise
1. A right or privilege conferred by law, such as a state charter authorizing the formation and existence of corporations.
2. The private contractual right to operate a business using a designated trade name and the operating procedures of a parent company (the franchisor).

fraud Any form of deceit, trickery, breach of confidence, or misrepresentation by which one party attempts to gain some unfair or dishonest advantage over another.

Freddie Mac A federally chartered corporation established as the Federal Home Loan Mortgage Corporation (FHLMC) for the purpose of purchasing mortgages in the secondary market, especially to accommodate savings association needs.

free and clear title Title to real property that is absolute and unburdened by any liens, mortgages, clouds, or other encumbrances.

freehold An estate in real property, the exact termination date of which is unknown (for a described yet indefinite period of time); those estates that have a potentially indefinite duration (fee simple) or a period of years incapable of exact determination (life estate).

freeholder One who owns land that he or she can transfer without anyone's permission; the owner of a freehold estate.

freestanding building A building containing one business rather than a row of stores or businesses with a common roof and side walls.

frontage The length of a property abutting a street or body of water, that is, the number of feet that front the street or water.

frontage street A street that is parallel and adjacent to a major street providing access to abutting properties but protected from heavy through traffic.

front foot A measurement of property frontage abutting the street line or waterfront line, with each front foot presumed to extend the depth of the lot.

front money The amount of hard money (cash as opposed to borrowed monies) the developer must have ready in order to purchase the land and to pay attorney fees, loan charges, and other initial expenses before actually developing the project.

fructus industriales Annual plantings and harvestable crops that require cultivation and are generally classified as personal property.

fructus naturales Uncultivated crops and perennial plantings, such as trees and bushes, which are generally classified as real property.

full disclosure A requirement to reveal fully and accurately all material facts, a requirement based on the theory that no fraud is committed if the purchaser has accurate and full information regarding the property to be purchased.

functional obsolescence A loss in value of an improvement due to functional inadequacies, often caused by age, poor design, or on the changing requirements of the buying public and may involve features that are unfashionable or unnecessary, such as a kitchen without modern built-in cabinets and sinks.

funding fee A fee paid to secure certain types of mortgage protection, such as the fee paid to the Department of Veterans Affairs for the VA to guarantee a veteran's loan.

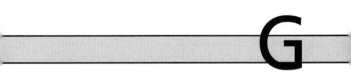

gain Profit received upon the sale of an asset.

gap financing The financing used to make up the difference between the underlying loan (floor loan) and the total amount required, usually filling a temporary need until permanent financing is obtained, sometimes called a *bridge loan* or *swing loan*.

gap in title A break in the chain of title, such as when the records do not reflect any transfer to a particular grantor.

garnishment A legal process designed to provide a means for creditors to safeguard their interest in a debtor's personal property that is in the hands of a third party (garnishee).

general agent One authorized by a principal to perform any and all acts associated with the continued operation of a particular job or a certain business of the principal; an essential feature of a general agency is the continuity of service, such as that provided by a property manager.

general contractor A construction specialist who enters into a formal construction contract with a developer to construct a real estate building or project; also called the prime contractor, a person who negotiates individual contracts with various subcontractors.

general improvement district A local public entity, such as a water district, created to perform a specific governmental function.

general lien The right of a creditor to have all the debtor's property, real and personal, sold to satisfy a debt.

general partner A co-owner of a partnership who is empowered to enter into contracts on behalf of the partnership and be fully liable for all partnership debts.

general partnership A form of business organization in which two or more co-owners carry on a business for profit and who share a full liability for the debts and obligations of the partnership.

general plan A long-range governmental program to regulate the use and development of property in an orderly fashion; a plan aimed at a well-balanced community growth.

Generation X A term used in demographics, the social sciences, and more broadly in popular culture to define persons born in the 1960s and 1970s.

General Services Administration (GSA) An independent agency organized in 1949 to manage, lease, and sell buildings belonging to the U.S. government.

geodetic survey system Refers to the United States Coast and Geodetic Survey System, the skeleton of which consists of a network of bench marks covering the entire country.

gift deed A deed in which the consideration is "love and affection," not supported by valuable consideration.

gift letter A letter provided to a lender or government agency acknowledging that the money being used (often, the down payment) to purchase real property was a gift from a relative and carries no obligation to repay.

gift tax A graduated federal tax paid by a donor upon making certain gifts.

G

Ginnie Mae A federal agency created in 1968 as a corporation without capital stock and as a division of HUD operating the special assistance aspects of federally aided housing programs including the management and liquidating functions of the old FNMA.

good consideration A consideration founded on love and affection for kindred by blood or marriage, which may be found in a gift deed but which is not sufficient to support a contract.

good faith Bona fide; an act is done in good faith if it is in fact done honestly, whether negligently or not.

good-faith estimate (GFE) A preliminary accounting of expected closing costs that provides enough information for the consumer to shop around for the best loan and terms; required by The Real Estate Settlement Procedures Act to be given to loan applicants within three business days of the completed loan application.

goodwill An intangible, salable asset arising from the reputation of a business; the expectation of continued public patronage; includes other intangible assets like trade name and going concern value.

government forces In appraisal theory, one of four forces affecting real estate value, e.g., government controls and regulations, public services, zoning, and building codes. The other three forces are environmental, economic, and social.

Government National Mortgage Association (GNMA) See **Ginnie Mae.**

government survey method A system of land description that applies to much of the land in the United States (over 30 states), particularly in the western states; also called the geodetic or rectangular survey system, and based on pairs of principal meridians and base lines, with each pair governing the surveys in a designated area.

grace period An agreed-on time after an obligation is past due during which a party can perform without being considered in default.

grade The elevation of a hill, road, sidewalk, or slope to the degree that it is inclined from level ground.

graduated payment mortgage (GPM) A mortgage in which the monthly payment for principal and interest graduates by a certain percentage each year for a specific number of years and then levels off for the remaining term of the mortgage, a program especially attractive to persons just starting their careers and anticipating increases in their incomes permitting them to obtain a home with initially a lower monthly installment obligation than would be available under a level payment plan.

graduated rental lease A lease in which the rent payments commence at a fixed, often low, rate but increase at set intervals as the lease term matures, often permitting long-term commercial tenants an opportunity to get started in business without a heavy financial burden during the early years.

grandfather clause A common expression used to convey the idea that something that was once permissible continues to be permissible despite changes in the controlling law.

grant The act of conveying or transferring title to real property.

grant deed A type of deed in which grantors warrant that they have not previously conveyed the estate being granted to another, that they have not encumbered the property except as noted in the deed, and that they will convey to a grantee any title to the property they may later acquire.

grantee The person who receives from the grantor a conveyance of real property.

grantor The person transferring title to, or an interest in, real property.

grantor-grantee index Public record books maintained in the official recorder's office, listing all recorded instruments and the liber (book) and page numbers where the complete and exact document can be found in the record books.

gratuitous agent An agent who receives no compensation for his or her services.

grid system The state-sponsored survey points to which metes-and-bounds surveys can be referenced; also called coordinate system.

grievance period A specified day or group of days during which the public may register complaints about tax assessments or other problems on the local level.

gross area The total floor area of a building, measured from the exterior of its walls (excluding uncovered areas such as courtyards or patios).

gross income The total income derived from a business, wages, or from income-producing property before adjustments or deductions for expenses, depreciation, taxes, and similar allowances.

gross income multiplier A numerical factor that expresses the relationship of gross income to sales price or value, calculated by dividing price by gross annual income.

gross lease A lease of property under which the lessee pays a fixed rent and the lessor pays the taxes, insurance, and other charges regularly incurred through ownership; also called a fixed or flat lease.

gross rent multiplier A rule of thumb for estimating the market value of income-producing residential property, derived by using comparable sales divided by the actual or estimated monthly rentals to arrive at an acceptable average.

ground area The area of a building computed from the exterior dimensions of the ground floor.

ground lease A lease of land alone, also called a land lease, used to separate the ownership of the land from the ownership of the buildings and improvements constructed on the land; usually a net lease that creates a tenancy for years, typically for a term of 55, 75, or 99 years.

group boycott A type of antitrust violation in which several brokers agree to refuse to cooperate or to cooperate on less favorable terms with a third broker, often in response to that broker's offering a discount brokerage program.

growing equity mortgage (GEM) A full-term mortgage with an initial payment and interest rate generally equal to the prevailing conventional market rate, with provisions for gradually increasing payments that are applied directly to principal thus substantially reducing both the term of the loan and the total amount of interest paid.

guaranteed mortgage certificate (GMC) A debt instrument issued by Freddie Mac, to raise money for its activities in the secondary market.

guaranty A pledge or security made by one person (the guarantor) to ensure that another person (the obligor) will perform his or her contract or fulfill his or her obligations to a third person (the obligee).

guardian A person, appointed by court or by will, given the lawful custody and care of the person or property of another (called a *ward*) who might be a minor, an insane person, or even a spendthrift.

H

habendum clause That part of a deed beginning with the words *to have and to hold,* following the granting clause, and reaffirming the extent of ownership that the grantor is transferring.

habitable Being in a condition that is fit to live in.

habitable room A room used for living purposes, such as a den, bedroom, or kitchen, as opposed to a bathroom or hallway.

handicap A protected class under the fair housing laws and the Americans with Disabilities Act (ADA) consisting of a physical or mental imairment that substantially limits one or more major life activities (walking, seeing, learning, working) or a record of having such an impairment or being regarded as having such impairment. It does not include current illegal use of or addiction to a controlled substance, but a person who is rehabilitated in these areas may be protected. The preferred word is "disability."

hard money mortgage Any mortgage loan given to a borrower in exchange for cash, as opposed to a mortgage given to finance a specific real estate purchase.

hazard insurance A property insurance policy that indemnifies against loss resulting from physical damage to property due to hazards such as fire, flood, and windstorm.

H

hazardous substance Any material that poses a threat to the environment or to public health, including substances that are toxic (lead to death), corrosive (acidic), ignitable (danger from heat or smoke), or reactive (can lead to explosions).

hazardous waste Materials that are inherently dangerous to handle or dispose of and are regulated by the EPA, including radioactive materials, certain chemicals, explosives, or biological waste.

hearing An administrative legal proceeding with definite issues of fact to be determined and with the parties having the right to be heard and have counsel present much the same as at a trial, although the rules of evidence are usually less strict than in a trial.

heavy industry Businesses that require ample property to accommodate their nature and function, such as factories, packing plants, or mills.

heir A person who inherits under a will or a person who succeeds to property by the state laws of descent if the decedent dies without a will (intestate).

heirs and assigns Heirs are recipients of an inheritance from a deceased owner, whereas assigns are successors in interest to a property; *heirs and assigns* are customarily inserted in deeds and wills and are considered to be words of limitation, not words of purchase.

hereditament Every kind of inheritable property, including real, personal, corporeal, and incorporeal; those things appurtenant to the land.

hidden risk A title risk that cannot be ascertained from an examination of the public records.

highest and best use An appraisal term meaning that reasonable and legal use, at the time of the property appraisal, which is most likely to produce the greatest net return to the land and/or the building over a given period of time.

high-water mark That line on the shore reached by the shoreward limit of the rise of medium tides and in most states, this mark, also called mean high water, is the seaward boundary of privately owned lands and the dividing line between public and private property.

historic structure A property listed in the National Register of Historic Places, located in a registered historic district and certified by the Secretary of the Interior as being of historic significance to the district, or located in a historic district designated under an appropriate state or local government statute that has been certified by the Department of the Interior and often provided certain tax incentives and deterrents to encourage the preservation of historic buildings and structures.

holdback

1. The portion of a loan commitment that will not be funded until some additional requirement has been attained, such as presale or rental of 70 percent of the units or completion of all building work.
2. In construction or interim financing, a percentage of the contractor's draw held back until satisfactory completion of the contractor's work and assurance of no mechanic's or materialman's liens.

hold-harmless clause A contract provision whereby one party agrees to indemnify and protect the other party from any injuries or lawsuits arising out of the particular transaction.

holding company A company that owns, directs, or controls the operations of one or more other corporations, usually directly owned subsidiaries; a corporation organized to hold the stock of other corporations, such as a bank holding company.

holding escrow An arrangement whereby an escrow agent holds the final title documents to a contract for deed.

holding period The period during which a person retains ownership of a capital asset.

holdover tenant A person who stays on the leased premises after his or her lease has expired.

holographic will A will written, dated, and signed in the testator's handwriting, but not witnessed and which may be valid in some states.

home equity line-of-credit loan A mortgage loan (usually in a subordinate position) that allows the borrower to obtain multiple advances of the loan proceeds at the borrower's discretion, up to an amount that represents a specific percentage of the borrower's equity in a property.

home inspection A professional inspection of a property to ascertain the condition of the improvements.

home loan A loan secured by a residence for one, two, three, or four families under either a mortgage or a deed of trust.

Home Mortgage Disclosure Act A federal law that requires lenders with federally related loans to disclose the number of loan applications and loans made in different parts of their service areas; designed to eliminate the discriminatory practice of redlining.

homeowners' association (HOA) A nonprofit association of homeowners organized pursuant to a declaration of restrictions or protective covenants for a subdivision, PUD, or condominium.

home ownership The status of owning the residence in which one lives.

homeowners' insurance A combined property and liability insurance policy designed for residential use, never including rising water, i.e., flooding, for which a separate policy must be purchased.

Homeowners' Warranty Program (HOW) A private insurance program that offers a buyer of a new home a ten-year warranty against certain physical defects, such as faulty roofing, heating, electrical services, and plumbing.

H

home rule The power of local governments to adopt zoning and building ordinances, as well as other land-use regulations.

homestead A tract of land that is owned and occupied as the family home.

homogeneous An appraisal term meaning of the same or similar kind.

horizontal property acts The name generally given to the body of laws pertaining to condominiums that permit ownership of a specified horizontal layer of airspace, as opposed to the traditional method of vertical ownership of property from the earth below to the sky above.

hostile possession Possession of real property by one person that is in contradiction, or adverse, to the possession of the title owner.

hotel As defined in many zoning codes, a building or group of attached or detached buildings containing lodging units and a lobby, clerk's desk, or counter with 24-hour clerk service and facilities for registration and keeping of records relating to hotel guests.

house rules
1. Rules of conduct adopted by the board of directors of a condominium owners' association and designed to promote harmonious living among the owners and occupants.
2. Rules of conduct specified by landlords of apartment buildings that must be fair and apply equally to all tenants.

housing for the elderly A project specifically designed for elderly persons (62 years of age or older), which provides living-unit accommodations and common-use space for social and recreational activities and, when needed, incidental facilities and space for health and nursing services for the project residents.

housing starts Housing units actually under construction, as distinguished from building permits issued.

HUD A federal cabinet department officially known as the U.S. Department of Housing and Urban Development, HUD is active in national housing programs. Among its many programs are urban renewal, public housing, model cities, rehabilitation loans, FHA-subsidy programs, and water and sewer grants.

HUD Code A standard for the construction of all manufactured homes created by the National Manufactured Housing Construction and Safety Standards Act of 1974 (also known as *Red Label*).

HUD-1 Form A form used at closings for all loans that are federally related, including FHA, VA, FDIC-insured funds, and any loans that will be sold to Fannie Mae or Freddie Mac. Exempt closings include cash sales, assumed loans, and seller-financed loans (carryback financing).

HVAC An acronym for the heating, ventilation, and air-conditioning systems in a building.

hypothecate To pledge specific real or personal property as security for an obligation without surrendering possession of it.

identity theft The deliberate act of assuming another's person's identity by using that person's information, such as birth date, Social Security number, address, name, and bank account information in order to gain access to the person's credit.

illiquidity Difficulty in selling an asset for full value on short notice.

illiterate A person who has not learned to read or write; an illiterate may still enter into contracts.

immediate family member In lenders' terms, the borrower's spouse, parent, stepparent, legal guardian, grandparent, brother, sister, or child.

impact fees A municipal assessment against new residential, industrial, or commercial development projects to compensate for the added costs of public services generated by the new construction.

implied agency An actual agency that arises by deduction or inference from other facts and circumstances, including the words and conduct of the parties.

implied contract An unwritten contract inferred from the actions of the parties.

implied easement An easement arising by implication from the acts or conduct of the parties.

implied listing A listing that arises by operation of law as implied from the acts of the parties; in most states, a listing must be in writing to be enforceable.

implied warranty of habitability A legal doctrine that imposes a duty on the landlord to make the leased premises habitable and ready for occupancy and continue to maintain them in a state of repair throughout the entire term of the lease.

impound account A trust account, also called an escrow account, established to set aside funds for future needs relating to a parcel of real property.

improved land Real property whose value has been enhanced by the addition of such on-site and off-site improvements as roads, sewers, utilities, and buildings, as distinguished from raw land.

improvements Valuable additions made to property that amount to more than repairs; cost of labor, and capital; and are intended to enhance the value of the property or extend the useful remaining life.

imputed notice An agent's knowledge that is binding on the principal because of the agency relationship between them.

inactive license A real estate license in inactive status.

inclusionary zoning A land-use concept in which local zoning ordinances require residential developers to include a certain percentage of dwelling units for low-income and moderate-income households as a condition to governmental approval of development of the project.

income and expense report A monthly financial report showing the income from the property, operating expenses, and the amount distributed to the owner.

income approach An approach to the valuation or appraisal of real property as determined by the amount of net income the property will produce over its remaining economic life; the market value is equal to the present worth of future net income.

income property   Property purchased primarily its potential to derive.

incompetent   A person who is not legally qualified to perform a valid act; one who lacks the power to act with legal effectiveness; any person who is impaired by reason of mental illness, physical disability, drugs, age, or other cause to the extent that he or she lacks sufficient understanding or capacity to make or communicate responsible decisions concerning his or her person.

incorporate   To form a corporation by preparing the necessary articles of incorporation and filing them with the appropriate state government business registration division.

incorporeal rights   Intangible or nonpossessory rights in real property, such as easements, licenses, profits, mining claims, insurance claims, and future rents; possessing no physical body.

incubator space   An industrial park building divided into small units of different sizes to accommodate young, growing companies that want to combine office and industrial space at one location.

incurable obsolescence An appraisal term meaning the external or functional obsolescence of an improvement that is not economically feasible to repair or correct.

indemnification An agreement to reimburse or compensate someone for a loss.

independent appraisal An appraisal conducted by a qualified, disinterested person.

independent contractor One retained to perform a certain act, but subject to the control and direction of another only as to the end result and not as to how he or she performs the act. Under IRS Section 3508, real estate licensees may be treated as independent contractors for income tax purposes only so long as three conditions exist: (1) a written contract, (2) a real estate license, and (3) payment of the salesperson on the basis of performance, not the number of hours worked.

index lease A lease that provides for adjustments of rent according to changes in a price index that is reliable and bears a close relationship to the nature of the tenant's business.

index rate The rate to which the interest rate on an adjustable-rate loan is tied.

indicated value The worth of a subject property as shown in the three approaches to value: (1) recent sales of comparable properties; (2) cost now less accrued depreciation plus land value; and (3) capitalization of annual net operating income.

indirect costs Development costs not related to the land or structure, such as legal and architectural fees, financing, and insurance costs during construction.

individual retirement account (IRA) A retirement savings program that can be either an "individual retirement account" or an "individual retirement annuity" from which first-time homebuyers (i.e., buyers who haven't owned a home in the past two years) can withdraw up to $10,000 from a retirement account free of the 10 percent penalty but not the burden of paying taxes to apply toward the down payment and closing costs.

indoor air quality (IAC) The presence of air pollutants inside a building.

industrial broker A real estate broker who specializes in brokering industrial real estate.

industrial park An area zoned for industrial use that contains sites for many separate industries and is developed and managed as a unit, usually with provisions for common services to its users.

inflation guard An endorsement to an insurance policy that automatically increases coverage during the life of the policy at a certain percentage per quarter, as selected by the insured.

informed consent Consent to a certain act that is given after a full and fair disclosure of all facts needed to make a conscious choice.

ingress A way to enter a property; access. The opposite of egress.

inheritance tax A state "estate" tax imposed on heirs for their right to inherit property.

in-house sale A sale in which the listing broker is the only broker in the transaction; there is no outside broker involved as in a cooperative sale.

initials An abbreviation for a name that is effective as a person's signature so long as the signer intends them to be equivalent to his or her legal signature.

injunction A legal action whereby a court issues a writ that forbids a party defendant from doing some act or compels the defendant to perform an act.

innocent misrepresentation A misstatement of material fact given without any intent to deceive.

inquiry notice Legal notice presumed by law when factors exist that would make a reasonable person inquire further.

inside lot Any lot located between the corner lots on a given block; an interior lot.

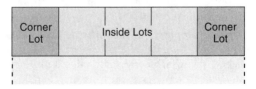

inspection A visit to and review of particular premises.

installment note A promissory note providing for payment of the principal in two or more indefinite stated amounts at different times.

installment sale For income tax purposes, a method of reporting gain received from the sale of real estate when the sales price is paid in installments, i.e., where at least one payment is to be received after the close of the taxable year in which the sale occurs.

institutional lender A financial institution such as a bank, insurance company, savings and loan association, or any lending institution whose loans are regulated by law.

instrument A formal legal document such as a contract, deed, or will.

insurable interest A right or interest in property that would cause the person who has that right or interest to suffer a monetary loss if the property were destroyed or damaged.

insurable title A title on which a title insuring company is willing to issue its policy of insurance.

insurance Indemnification against loss from a specific hazard or peril.

intangible property Anything having no material or physical existence or that cannot be seen or touched; that which derives any value it may have from what it represents, such as the "bundle of rights."

interest The sum paid or accrued in return for the use of money.

interest in property A legal share of ownership in property, whether the entire ownership (as in a fee simple interest) or partial ownership (as in a leasehold estate).

interest-only mortgage loans A mortgage loan under which the borrower only pays the interest on the loan for a period of time, often five to seven years, after which the borrower either pays off the loan in full, refinances, or starts to pay off the principal.

interest rate cap The maximum interest rate charge allowed on an adjustable-rate loan for any one adjustment period during the life of the loan; the loan may also have a lifetime cap on interest.

Internet A world-wide electronic network connecting government, academic, and business institutions providing data, news, and opinions.

interim financing A short-term loan usually made during the construction phase of a building project; often referred to as a *construction loan* and usually disbursing proceeds in increments as the construction progresses.

interim use The uses to which sites and improved properties may be put until they are ready for a more productive highest and best use.

intermediate theory The legal concept that a mortgage is a lien on a property until default, at which time title passes to the lender.

internal rate of return (IRR) A rate of discount at which the present worth of future cash flows is exactly equal to the initial capital investment.

Internal Revenue Code of 1986 (IRC) The body of statutes codifying the federal tax laws and administered by the Internal Revenue Service (IRS), an agency that issues its own regulations interpreting those laws.

interpleader A legal proceeding whereby an innocent third party (stakeholder), such as an escrow agent or broker, can deposit with the court property or money that he or she holds and that is subject to adverse claims so that the court can distribute it to the rightful claimant.

interstate An event occurring between two or more states, thus triggering the jurisdiction of federal law such as the federal securities laws.

Interstate Land Sales Full Disclosure Act A federal law that regulates interstate land sales by requiring registration of real property with the Office of Interstate Land Sales Registration (OILSR) of the U.S. Department of Housing and Urban Development (HUD) to provide disclosure of full and accurate information regarding the property to prospective buyers before they decide to buy.

interval ownership A popular system of time-share ownership in which the owner acquires title to a specific unit for a certain week (or weeks) of each year.

inter vivos trust A "living" trust, which takes effect during the life of the creator, as opposed to a testamentary trust, which is created within a person's will and does not take effect until the death of the creator.

intestate Dying without a will or having left a will that is defective in form causing the decedent's property to pass to his or her heirs according to the laws of descent in the state where such real property is located.

intrinsic value An appraisal term meaning the result of a person's individual choices and preferences for a given geographical area based on the features and amenities the area has to offer.

inventory
1. An itemized list of property.
2. A list of goods on hand held for sale in the ordinary course of business.

inverse condemnation An action for just compensation brought by a person whose property has been effectively taken, substantially interfered with, or taken without just compensation.

involuntary conversion A tax term referring to loss of property through destruction or condemnation.

involuntary lien A lien created by operation of law, such as a real property tax lien, judgment lien, or mechanic's lien.

irrevocable consent An agreement that cannot be withdrawn or revoked.

irrigation districts Quasi-political districts created under special state laws to provide water services to property owners in the district and given the power to levy assessments to finance the districts' operations.

J

joint and several liability A situation in which more than one party is liable for repayment of a debt or obligation and a creditor can obtain compensation from one or more parties, either individually or jointly.

joint tenancy An estate or unit of interest in real estate that is owned by two or more natural persons all owning equal shares with rights of survivorship; the death of one joint tenant simply reduces by one the number of persons who jointly own the unit. Four unities are required to create a joint tenancy: unity of title, unity of time, unity of interest, and unity of possession.

joint venture The joining of two or more people in a specific business enterprise, such as the development of a condominium project or a shopping center.

judgment The formal decision of a court on the respective rights and claims of the parties to an action or suit that, once entered and recorded with the county recorder, usually becomes a general lien on the property of the defendant.

judgment lien A purely statutory general lien on real and personal property belonging to a debtor.

judgment-proof Having no assets to satisfy a judgment for money.

judicial foreclosure A method of foreclosing on real property by means of a court-supervised sale.

judicial precedent A legal term describing the requirements established by prior court decisions (called case law).

jumbo loan A residential mortgage loan that exceeds the loan amounts acceptable for sale to Freddie Mac and Fannie Mae.

junior mortgage A mortgage, such as a second mortgage, that is subordinate in right or lien priority to an existing mortgage on the same realty.

jurisdiction The authority or power to act, such as the authority of a court to hear and render a decision that binds both parties.

just compensation An amount of compensation to be received by a party for the taking of his or her property under the power of eminent domain.

J

K

key lot A lot that has added value because of its strategic location, especially when needed for the highest and best use of contiguous property; a lot that adjoins the rear property line of a corner lot and fronts on a secondary street; the piece of property that is essential to the development of a project.

key tenant A major office building tenant that leases several floors; a major department store in a shopping center.

L

land The surface of the earth extending down to its center and upward to the sky, including all natural things thereon such as trees, crops, or water, plus the minerals below the surface and the air rights above.

land contract An installment contract for sale with the buyer receiving equitable title (right to possession) and the seller retaining legal title (record title).

landlocked Real property that has no legal access to a public road or way.

landlord The lessor or the owner of leased premises who retains a reversionary interest in the property; when the lease ends, the property reverts to the landlord.

landmark A stake, stream, cliff, monument, or other object or feature used to fix or define land boundaries.

landlease communities A community or a parcel of land containing two or more manufactured homes in which the homeowner rents the land on which the manufactured home is situated.

land trust A trust originated by the owner of real property in which real estate is the only asset.

land-use intensity A system of land use under local zoning codes or comprehensive development ordinances designed to relate land, building coverage of the land, and open space to one another.

land-use map A map that shows the types and intensities of different land uses.

land-use plan A plan submitted to a local government agency by a developer of a proposed real estate project as part of the permitting process under local comprehensive development ordinances.

late charge An added charge a borrower is required to pay for failure to pay a regular loan installment when due.

latent defects Hidden structural defects presumably resulting from faulty construction, known to the seller but not to the purchaser, and not readily discoverable by inspection. Failure to disclose such information is a tacit misrepresentation and grounds for the buyer to rescind the contract.

law That body of rules by which society governs itself. Real estate law derives from state and federal constitutions, state and federal legislation, regulations of federal and state boards and commissions, county and municipal ordinances, and, most important, court decisions. *Private law* refers to the law that the parties create for themselves in their legal documents, such as the private rules of conduct for the owners that the bylaws and house rules of a condominium set forth, and the legal recourse available for violating these rules.

L

lawful interest The maximum interest rate permitted by law, with any amount above the statutory rate deemed usurious.

Lead-Based Paint Hazard Reduction Act (LBPHRA) A federal law, effective in 1996, outlining a comprehensive federal strategy for reducing lead paint hazard exposure. The act and enabling regulations require affirmative action on the part of the sellers, landlords, real estate agents, and renovators disturbing more than two square feet of old paint in houses built before 1978 to ensure that lead-based paint hazards are addressed in the sale and leasing of these homes and apartments. Each tenant or buyer must be given the HUD booklet

"Protect Your Family from Lead in Your Home." The law does not require testing, removal, or abatement. The buyer, although not the tenant, must be given the opportunity to test for lead-based paint within ten days or any time agreed upon, or the opportunity may be waived altogether. Real estate agents are responsible for ensuring seller/lessor compliance under the regulations. Failure to do so can result in fines up to $11,000 per omission.

lease An agreement, written or unwritten, transferring the right to exclusive possession and use of real estate for a definite period of time. The lessor (landlord) grants the right of possession to the lessee (tenant) but retains the right to retake possession after the lease term has expired (reversionary right).

The requirements for a valid lease are similar to those of a contract and are generally as follows: capacity to contract; mutual agreement; legal objectives; statute of frauds; signatures of the parties; description and use of the premises; term; possession; consideration. Leases may be terminated by expiration, merger, destruction, abandonment, agreement of the parties, forfeiture, or commercial frustration of purpose.

leasehold A less-than-freehold estate that a tenant possesses in real property; four principal leasehold types include an estate for years, the periodic tenancy (estate from year to year), the tenancy at will, and the tenancy at sufferance.

leasehold improvements The improvements to leased property made by the lessee.

lease option A lease clause that gives the tenant the right to purchase the property under specified conditions.

lease purchase agreement An agreement in which part of the rent payment is applied toward a set purchase price, and title is transferred from lessor to lessee when the lessor receives the pre-arranged total price.

legacy A disposition of money or personal property by will, as in a bequest. The recipient is called the *legatee*.

legal age The statutory age at which a person attains majority and is no longer a minor.

legal description A description of a piece of real property that is acceptable by the courts of the state where the property is located for use in real property conveyance documents and which is complete enough that an independent surveyor can locate and identify that specific parcel of land.

legally permissible Use of property that is allowable by law, as required in the highest-and-best-use analysis.

legal name The given name in combination with the surname or family name.

legal notice Notice that is either implied or required by law as a result of the possession of property or the recording of documents.

legal rate of interest The rate of interest prescribed by state law that prevails in the absence of any agreement fixing the rate.

lessee The person to whom property is rented or leased; called a *tenant* in most residential leases.

lessor The person who rents or leases property to another. In residential leasing, he or she is often referred to as a *landlord*.

less-than-freehold estate The estate held by a person who rents or leases property.

let To rent out.

letter of credit An agreement or commitment by a bank (issuer) made at the request of a customer (account party) that the bank honor drafts or other demands of payment from third parties (beneficiaries) upon compliance with the conditions specified in the letter of credit.

letter of intent An expression of intent to invest, develop, or purchase without creating any firm legal obligation to do so.

letter report A short appraisal report limited to the property characteristics, valuation, and recommendations.

A report by a title company as to the condition of title as of a specific date; it gives no insurance on that title, however.

level-payment mortgage A mortgage scheduled for repayment in equal periodic payments that include both principal and interest.

leverage The impact of borrowed funds on investment return.

levy To assess; to seize or collect.

liability
1. In a double-entry accounting system, all amounts appearing on the credit side, including all amounts owed.
2. Legal responsibility for an act.

license Permission or authority to do a particular act on the land or property of another, usually on a nonexclusive basis.

Formal permission from a constituted authority (such as a state real estate commission) to engage in a certain activity or business (such as real estate brokerage or real estate appraisal).

licensee A person who has a valid real estate or appraisal license.

license laws Laws enacted by all states, the District of Columbia, and certain Canadian provinces that provide the states with the authority to license and regulate the activities of real estate brokers, salespeople, and appraisers. The general purposes of license laws are to (1) protect the public from dishonest or incompetent real estate practitioners; (2) prescribe certain standards and qualifications for licensing; and (3) raise the standards of the real estate profession.

lien A charge or claim that one person (lienor) has on the property of another (lienee) as security for a debt or obligation; priority is normally determined by the date of recordation.

lien statement A statement of the unpaid balance of a promissory note secured by a lien on property, plus the status of interest payments, maturity date, and any claims that may be asserted.

lien-theory states Those states that treat a mortgage solely as a security interest in the secured real property with title retained by the mortgagor, allowing the mortgagor use of the property and all rents and profits.

life estate Any estate in real or personal property that is limited in duration to the life of its owner or the life of some other designated person; created by agreement of the parties (*conventional life estate*) or by operation of law (homestead, curtesy, or dower), referred to as a *legal life estate;* and terminated by the death of the person whose existence is the measuring life.

life tenant A person possessing a life estate.

light industry A zoning designation for industrial use encompassing mostly unobjectionable light manufacturing, as opposed to those industries that cause noise, air, or water disturbances and pollution.

like-kind property A federal term relating to the nature of real estate rather than its quality or quantity; like-kind property qualifies for a real estate exchange and the resulting tax benefit.

limitations of actions Time within which legal actions must be commenced or else action is barred.

limited access highway A highway with access only at specific intervals, usually by way of ramps.

limited common elements That special class of common elements in a condominium project that is reserved for the use of one or more apartment(s) to the exclusion of other apartments.

limited liability company (LLC) An alternative, hybrid business entity with the combined characteristics and benefits of both limited partnerships and S corporations. Unlike a corporation, an LLC does not have perpetual existence.

limited partnership A partnership agreement in which one person (called the *general partner*) or group of persons organizes, operates, and is responsible for the entire partnership venture. The others are *limited partners,* and these investors have no say in the organization and direction of the operation, but share in the profits, and compensate the general partner for his or her efforts out of such profits.

limited power of attorney A power of attorney that is restricted to a particular task, such as the transfer of a specific parcel of property.

limited referral agent A salesperson with an active real estate license who refers prospective buyer or seller leads into the brokerage company in return for a referral fee upon closing.

listing   **145**

limited service broker A broker who offers the consumer less than the full line of services usually provided by a real estate broker.

limited warranty deed A deed that contains warranties covering the time period the grantor holds title.

line of credit The maximum amount of money a bank will lend one of its more reliable and credit-worthy customers without the need for a formal loan submission.

line-of-sight easement A right that restricts the use of land within the easement area in any way that interferes with the view.

liquidated damages An amount predetermined by the parties to an agreement as the total amount of compensation an injured party should receive if the other party breaches a specified part of the contract.

liquidity The ability to sell an asset and convert it into cash at a price close to its true value.

lis pendens (Lis/P) A recorded legal document that gives constructive notice that an action affecting a particular piece of property has been filed in a state or federal court.

listing A written employment agreement between a property owner and a real estate broker authorizing the broker to find a buyer or a tenant for certain real property. Listings can take the form of open listings, net listings, exclusive-agency listings, or exclusive-right-to-sell listings.

L

littoral land Land bordering on the shore of a sea or ocean and thus affected by the tide currents.

living trust An arrangement in which a property owner (trustor) transfers assets to a trustee who assumes specified duties in managing the asset.

loan balance table A table showing the balance remaining to be paid on an amortized loan; also called a remaining balance table.

loan commitment A written pledge by a lender to lend a certain amount of money to a qualified borrower on a particular piece of real estate for a specified time under specific terms.

loan pool A block of loans held in trust as collateral to support an issue of mortgage-backed securities.

loan pooler A company that assembles large blocks of loans to be held in trust as collateral for the issuance of a series of mortgage-backed securities.

loan submission A package of pertinent papers and documents regarding a specific property or properties that is received by a lender for review and consideration for the purpose of making a mortgage loan.

loan-to-value (LTV) ratio The ratio of a mortgage loan principal to the property's appraised value or its sales price, whichever is lower.

local improvement district A separate legal entity, activated under state law by the inhabitants of a particular geographic area.

locational obsolescence Loss of value caused by negative influence outside the property, for example, a commercial use abutting a residential property.

lock box A special lock placed on the door of a listed property designed to facilitate the broker's showing of that property.

lock-in clause
1. A condition in a promissory note that prohibits prepayment of the note.
2. A contract provision covering the right of buyer and seller to notify the lender to fix the amount of points as of the date of the notice.

loss factor A commercial leasing term, also known as the *load factor* or *partial floor factor,* which is the square-footage difference between the rentable area and the usable area expressed as a percentage.

L

loss payee The person designated on an insurance policy as the one to be paid in case the insured property is damaged or destroyed.

lot, block, and subdivision A description of real property that identifies a parcel of land by reference to lot and block numbers appearing on maps and plats of recorded subdivided land.

love and affection Usual consideration when a gift is intended.

lump-sum payment Repayment of a debt by a single payment, including principal and accrued interest.

M

Maggie Mae Nickname for the first nonfederal secondary market for conventional mortgages that provides a market where a lender can sell Mortgage Guaranty Insurance Corporation (MGIC)–insured mortgages to other investors.

magicwrap A mortgaging procedure in which MGIC insures a mortgage and sells it on the secondary market when the mortgage wraps around an existing VA or FHA mortgage.

maintenance The care and work put into a building to keep it in operation and productive use.

maintenance fee A charge or lien levied against property owners to maintain their real estate in operation and productive use, especially in condominiums.

majority The age at which a person is no longer a minor and is thus able to enter freely into contracts.

maker The person (borrower) who executes a promissory note and thus becomes primarily liable for payment to the payee (lender).

malfeasance Commission of an act that is clearly unlawful; especially applicable to acts of a public official.

management agreement A contract between the owner of income-producing property and the individual or firm that will manage that property, establishing the scope of the agent's authority, as well as duties, compensation, termination procedures, payment of expenses, and other matters.

management survey A detailed analysis of the economic, physical, and operational aspects of a property, with recommendations as to changes and improvements that could enhance the property's profitability.

manufactured housing A type of housing unit factory-constructed according to standards of the Federal Manufactured Home Construction and Safety Standards (HUD Title 6) on a permanent chassis and containing at least 320 square feet, and which, if properly sited, can be used as security for a mortgage loan that both Fannie Mae and Freddie Mac will purchase.

maps and plats Surveys of particular pieces of land showing monuments, boundaries, area, ownership, and the like, prepared by registered surveyors or civil engineers.

M

margin The amount added to the index rate that represents the lender's cost of doing business (includes costs, profits, and risk of loss of the loan) in an adjustable rate loan.

marginal land Land that is of little value because of some deficiency, such as poor access, inadequate rainfall, or steep terrain.

marginal release Notation of a satisfaction or release of mortgage by a county recorder, as evidenced by a note of its liber (book) and page number in the margin of the recorded mortgage.

marginal tax rate The ordinary rate of income tax charged on the last dollar of income; often used when making calculations for investment decisions.

mark A symbol used for a signature.

market A group of properties that would each be competitive to a given typical buyer.

marketable title Good or clear saleable title reasonably free from risk of litigation over possible defects; also referred to as *merchantable title*.

market conditions Features of the marketplace, including (but not limited to) interest rates, demographics, employment levels, vacancy rates, and absorption levels.

M

marketing period The period of time between the start of marketing and the final closing.

market value The most probable price a property should bring in a competitive and open market under all conditions requisite to a fair sale under guidelines published by federal lending institutions (Fannie Mae, Freddie Mac).

master deed The principal conveyance document used by the owners of land on which condominiums are located.

master form instrument An instrument containing various forms such as covenants and other clauses in a mortgage or deed of trust that may be recorded with the county registrar as a master form instrument.

master lease The dominant lease in a building or development.

master plan A comprehensive plan to guide the long-term physical development of a particular area.

material fact Any fact that is relevant to a person making a decision.

materialman The supplier of materials used in the construction of an improvement, and who is entitled to a lien on the property for monies overdue, whether they are due from the owner or the prime contractor.

maturity The time when a debt, such as a mortgage note, becomes due and is extinguished if paid in accordance with the agreed on schedule of payments.

mean The average of a set of numbers. The mean of 1, 3, 7, and 9 is 5.

M

meander line An artificial line used by surveyors to measure the natural, uneven, winding property line formed by rivers, streams, and other watercourses bordering a property.

mechanic's lien A statutory lien created in favor of materialmen and mechanics (and architects and designers in some states) to secure payment for materials supplied and services rendered in the improvement, repair, or maintenance of real property.

median The middle figure in a set of numbers.

mediation An alternative process of dispute resolution in which an independent third party works with two disputing parties to help them resolve their differences.

meeting of the minds Mutual assent or agreement between the parties to a contract regarding the substance of the contract.

menace The threat of violence used to obtain a contract; a ground to void a contract.

merger The uniting or combining of two or more interests or estates into one.

meridian One of a set of imaginary lines running north and south used by surveyors for reference in locating and describing land under the government survey method of property description.

metes and bounds A common method of land description that identifies a property by specifying the shape and boundary dimensions of the parcel, using terminal points and angles beginning and returning to the true point of beginning.

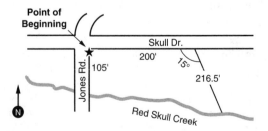

meth labs The places where illegal methamphetamines are manufactured. The by-products render the buildings and the grounds surrounding them more contaminated than many federally designated toxic waste sites.

metropolitan statistical area (MSA) The area in and around a major city.

middleman A person who brings two or more parties together but does not conduct negotiations.

military clause A provision in some residential leases allowing a tenant in military service to terminate the lease in case of transfer, discharge, or other appropriate circumstances.

mill One-tenth of one cent; some states use a mill rate to compute property taxes and sales taxes.

mineral rights Rights to subsurface land and profits.

minimum lot area A zoning ordinance requirement establishing a minimum lot size upon which a building may be erected.

M

minimum property requirements The minimum requirements for a property to be livable, soundly built, and suitably located as to site and neighborhood before the FHA will underwrite a residential mortgage loan.

minimum rent The smallest amount of rent from a tenant under a lease with a varying rent schedule; base rent.

ministerial acts Routine acts that can be performed for the customer without creating an agency relationship, although such actions may require a real estate license. Do not involve judgment, discretion, or advice.

miniwarehouse A structure containing self-storage units.

minor A person under the legal age of majority; a legal infant who is not a completely competent legal party.

minority A subgroup that appears to be outnumbered by other groups and often used to categorize people of a different language, sex, color, nationality, religion, culture, ethnicity, or lifestyle. In the context of fair housing laws, refers to consumers who have been discriminated against historically and for whom such discrimination is now prohibited. The preferred term today is *protected classes*.

misdemeanor A crime, less serious than a felony, usually punishable by fine or imprisonment for one year or less.

misnomer A mistake in a name.

misplaced improvement A poorly located or poorly planned improvement or one that does not conform to the best use of the site.

misrepresentation A false statement or concealment of a material fact made with the intention of inducing some action by another party; a court will grant relief in the form of damages or rescission if the misrepresented fact is material to the transaction.

mistake An error or misunderstanding, possibly rendering a contract voidable if the mistake is mutual, material, unintentional, and free from negligence.

mitigation Methods used to reduce the sources of environmental hazards and to limit their impact on the environment and human life.

mitigation of damages A principle of contract law referring to the obligation of an injured party to take reasonable steps to reduce or eliminate the amount of damages that party may be entitled to.

mixed use The use of real property for more than one use, such as a condominium building that has residential and commercial units.

mobile home Prefabricated trailer-type housing units built prior to June 15, 1976. This term is often incorrectly applied to manufactured housing.

mobile home park An area zoned and set up to accommodate manufactured (mobile) homes and provide water hookups and sewage disposal for each home.

model home A house built as part of a land development program to demonstrate style, construction, and possible furnishings of similar houses to be erected and sold.

Modified Accelerated Cost Recovery System (MARCS) A method of depreciation allowing for depreciating assets over a longer period; effective for property placed in service after December 31, 1986, the recovery period is 27.5 years for residential rental property and 39 years for non-residential real property.

modification
1. The influence on land use and value resulting from human made improvements to surrounding parcels.
2. A change to a contract. A contract can be modified at any time with the consent of both parties.
3. A change to a building design as required by law, such as a requirement under the Americans with Disabilities Act to make a public-accommodation building more accessible to persons with disabilities.

modification and assumption agreement A written agreement to change the interest rate when the due-on-sale provision of the mortgage is enforced upon a change of ownership, releasing the previous mortgagor from personal liability under the mortgage.

modular construction A highly engineered method of producing six-sided buildings (four walls plus a ceiling and floor) or building components in an efficient and cost-effective manner in a controlled manufacturing (factory) environment; also called prefabricated housing.

mold
1. The cornice; wood molding applied to cover the junction of roof boards and the outside wall.

2. A simple life form, lacking the ability to photosynthesize, that releases alcohols, ketones, and carbons, as well as spores, all of which can cause allergic, respiratory, and sinus problems in some people.

money market fund A form of mutual fund that trades primarily in short-term debt obligations, such as certificates of deposit (CDs), commercial paper, Treasury bills, and other U.S. government securities.

month-to-month tenancy A periodic tenancy whereby the tenant rents for one period at a time; the estate continues renewing for an indefinite period of time until either lessor or lessee gives the statutory notice of termination.

monument A visible marker, either a natural or artificial object, set by the government or surveyors, used to establish the lines and boundaries of a survey.

moral character The ability on the part of the person licensed to serve the general public in a fair and honest manner.

M

moral turpitude An act of baseness, vileness, or depravity in private social duties (that is, duties one owes to a fellow person or to society generally); contrary to the accepted customary rule of right and duty between persons; conduct contrary to justice, honesty, modesty, or good morals, such as embezzlement, perjury, robbery, and larceny.

moratorium
1. A temporary suspension of payments due under a financing agreement in order to help a distressed borrower recover and thus avoid a default and foreclosure.
2. A temporary suspension of issuing building permits pending governmental study of more restrictive zoning controls, as with condominium conversions.

more or less A phrase indicating that the dimension or size given is approximate when describing real property.

mortgage A legal document used to secure the performance of an obligation; a valid mortgage requires both a debt and a pledge and is extinguished only after the debt is paid.

mortgage-backed security (MBS) A security guaranteed by pools of mortgages and used to channel funds from securities markets to housing markets.

M

mortgage banker A person, corporation, or firm not otherwise in banking and finance that normally provides its own funds for mortgage financing as opposed to savings and loan associations or commercial banks that use other people's money—namely that of their depositors—to originate mortgage loans.

mortgage broker A person or firm that acts as an intermediary between borrower and lender; one who, for compensation or gain, negotiates, sells, or arranges loans and sometimes continues to service the loans; also called a **loan broker.**

mortgagee In a mortgage transaction, the party who receives and holds a mortgage as security for a debt; the lender; a lender or creditor who holds a mortgage as security for payment of an obligation.

mortgage insurance An insurance plan that pays off the mortgage balance in the event of the death or, in some plans, disability of the insured mortgagor.

mortgage lien A voluntary lien or charge on the property of a mortgagor that secures the underlying debt obligation.

mortgage pool A common fund of mortgage loans in which one can invest.

mortgagor The one who gives a mortgage as security for a debt; the borrower; usually the landowner, though it could be the owner of a leasehold estate; the borrower or debtor who hypothecates or puts up his or her property as security for an obligation.

M

motel A structure designed to provide convenient rental quarters for transients with parking provided at or near the room.

multiple-asset exchange An exchange of property for income tax purposes, usually involving two businesses, in which the values of many related assets—land, buildings, machinery, goodwill—are added together to reach a composite figure on which to compute the exchange.

multiple dwelling A structure used for the accommodation of two or more families or households in separate living units; an apartment building.

multiple listing service (MLS) A service in which member brokers pool their listings and offer cooperation and compensation to other member brokers usually owned and operated by a local association of REALTORS®, but not always.

mutual agreement The consent of all parties to the provisions of a contract; voluntary cancellation of a contract by all parties is called *mutual rescission*.

mutuality of consent A meeting of the minds; a mutual assent of the parties to the formation of the contract.

mutual mortgage insurance fund One of four FHA insurance funds into which all insurance premiums and other specified FHA revenues are paid, and from which any losses are met.

M

mutual savings banks Savings institutions that issue no stock and are mutually owned by their investors who are paid dividends, not interest, operating similarly to savings and loan associations and located primarily in the northeastern section of the United States.

mutual water company A water company organized by or for water users in a given district, with the object of securing an ample water supply at a reasonable rate.

naked title Bare title to the property, lacking the usual rights and privileges of ownership.

name, reservation of The exclusive right to the use of a trade name or a corporate name.

National Environmental Protection Act (NEPA) The 1969 law establishing the Environmental Protection Agency (EPA), which has developed programs and activities that affect, protect, and improve environmental quality.

National Flood Insurance Program (NFIP) A federal program created in 1968, managed by the Federal Emergency Management Agency (FEMA), which oversees floodplain management and mapping components of the program.

National Housing Partnership A private, profit-making company in conjunction with its sole and general partner and administrative arm, the National Corporation for Housing Partnership, which specializes in housing for low- to moderate-income families, the handicapped, and the elderly.

natural person An individual; a private person, as distinguished from an artificial entity such as a corporation or partnership.

navigable waters A body of saltwater or freshwater capable of carrying a commercial vessel and large enough to ebb and flow (a "highway for commerce").

negative amortization A financing arrangement in which the monthly payments are less than the true amortized amounts and the loan balance increases over the term of the loan rather than decreases; an interest shortage that is added to unpaid principal.

negative cash flow A situation in which cash expenditures to maintain an investment (taxes, mortgage payments, and maintenance) exceed the cash income received from the investment.

negative easement An easement, such as a building restriction or a view easement, that has the effect of preventing the servient landowner from doing an act otherwise permitted.

negligence The failure to use ordinary or reasonable care under the circumstances.

N

negotiable instrument Any written instrument that may be transferred by endorsement or delivery so as to vest legal title in the transferee, such as checks, publicly traded stocks, and promissory notes.

negotiation The transaction of business aimed at reaching a meeting of the minds among the parties; the act of bargaining.

neighborhood Contiguous areas showing common characteristics of population and homogeneity of land use.

neighborhood shopping center A group of retail buildings, usually 15 to 20, providing a variety of convenience stores, having common parking and management and catering to 1,000 or more families.

net after taxes The net operating income after deducting all charges, including federal and state income taxes.

net income The sum arrived at after deducting from gross income the expenses of a business or investment, including taxes, insurance, and allowances for vacancy and bad debts; generally calculated before accounting for depreciation.

net lease A lease, usually commercial, in which the lessee not only pays the rent for occupancy but also pays maintenance and operating expenses such as taxes, insurance, utilities, and repairs.

net listing An employment contract in which the broker receives as commission all excess monies over and above the minimum sales price agreed on by broker and seller; its use is discouraged or prohibited in most states.

N

net operating income (NOI) The balance remaining after deducting from gross receipts all fixed expenses, operating expenses, replacement reserves, and allowance for vacancy and bad debts, but before deducting any debt service, income taxes, or depreciation.

net proceeds The cash received after paying all liens and expenses.

net spendable income The money remaining each year after collecting rents and paying operating expenses and mortgage payments.

net usable acre That portion of a property that is suitable for building.

net worth The value remaining after deducting liabilities from assets.

net yield That portion of gross yield that remains after all costs—such as loan servicing and reserves—are deducted.

new town A modern concept of urban planning characterized by a development that offers a complete range of services including housing, recreation, schools, and churches, as well as a thoroughly planned and controlled balance of land use.

"no deal/no commission" clause A clause in a listing contract that stipulates a commission is to be paid *only if and when title passes*.

nominal consideration A consideration bearing no relation to the real value of a contract used so as not to reveal the true value of the property being conveyed; in name only, and not having any relation to actual market value.

nominal interest rate The stated interest rate in a note or contract, which may differ from the true or effective interest rate.

noncompetition clause A provision in a contract or lease prohibiting a person from operating or controlling a nearby business that would compete with one of the parties to the contract; also called a "no-compete" clause; enforceable as long as it is reasonable as to time and location.

nonconforming use A permitted use of real property that was lawfully established and maintained at the time of its original construction but that no longer conforms to the current zoning law.

nondisclosure The failure to reveal a fact, with or without the intention to conceal it.

nonhomogeneic The fact that all properties are unique, even similar houses in a tract subdivision, each with its own "bundle of rights."

nonjudicial foreclosure The process of selling real property under a power of sale in a mortgage or deed of trust that is in default.

nonprofit corporation A corporation formed for a nonprofit purpose, such as a charity or a political, fraternal, educational, or trade organization, covered by special tax rules found in IRC Section 501.

nonrecourse loan A loan in which the borrower is not held personally liable on the note.

normal wear and tear The physical deterioration that occurs with the normal use of a property without negligence, carelessness, accident with, or abuse of the premises, equipment, or chattels by the occupants or their guests.

notary public A public officer who functions as an official witness; whose duties include administering oaths; attesting to and certifying documents by his or her signature and official seal; and taking acknowledgments of deeds and other conveyances.

note A document signed by the borrower of a loan and stating the loan amount, the interest rate, the time and method of repayment, and the obligation to repay; serves as evidence of the debt.

notice Information that may be required by the terms of a contract.

notice of assessment A notice issued by the state or local taxing agency to the owner of real property specifying the assessed valuation of the property.

notice of completion A document filed in some states to give public notice that a construction job has been completed and that mechanics' liens must be filed within a specified time to be valid.

notice of consent A legal procedure that allows a state official to receive legal process for non-residents.

notice of default A notice to a defaulting party announcing that a default has occurred.

notice of dishonor A document issued by a notary public at the request of a note holder who has been refused payment of the note by its maker; serves legal evidence that the note is unpaid.

notice of lien A specific written notice required in some states in an application for a mechanic's lien.

notice of nonresponsibility A legal notice designed to relieve a property owner of responsibility for the cost of improvements ordered by another person (such as a tenant).

notice to quit A written notice given by a landlord to the tenant stating that the landlord intends to regain possession of the leased premises and that the tenant is required to leave and yield the property.

novation The substitution of a new obligation for an old one; substitution of new parties to an existing obligation, as when the parties to an agreement accept a new debtor in place of an old one.

N

nuisance Conduct or activity that results in an actual physical interference with another's reasonable use or enjoyment of his or her property for any lawful purpose.

null and void Having no legal force or effect, of no worth; unenforceable; not binding.

oath A solemn pledge made before a notary public or other officer.

obligor A promisor; one who incurs a lawful obligation to another (the obligee).

obsolescence A cause of depreciation in a property. Can be due to some structural defect (functional obsolescence), or may be loss in value from causes in the neighborhood but outside the property itself (external obsolescence).

occupancy agreement An agreement to permit the buyer to occupy the property before the close of escrow in consideration of paying the seller a specified rent, usually on a daily prorated basis.

occupancy permit A permit issued by the appropriate governing unit to establish that a property is habitable and meets necessary health and safety standards.

occupancy rate
1. The ratio of space rented relative to the amount of space available for rent.
2. The rent received divided by the income possible from full occupancy.

offer A promise by one party to act or perform in a specified manner provided the other party acts or performs in the manner requested.

offer and acceptance The two components of a valid contract; a meeting of the minds.

offeror The party who makes an offer to an offeree.

offer to sell Broadly defined in most condominium and subdivision statutes to include any inducement, solicitation, or attempt to encourage a person to buy property or acquire an interest in property.

office building A building usually divided into individual offices, used primarily by companies to conduct business.

Office of Equal Opportunity (OEO) The   federal agency under the direction of the Secretary of the Department of Housing and Urban Development that is in charge of administering the federal Fair Housing Act.

Office of Interstate Land Sales Registration (OILSR) The federal agency that regulates interstate land sales to prevent abuse, such as fraud and misrepresentation, perpetrated on the public in the promotion and sale of recreational property across state lines.

O

Office of the Comptroller of the Currency (OCC) A federal agency within the U.S. Treasury Department that regulates nationally chartered banks.

Office of Thrift Supervision (OTS) A branch of the U.S. Treasury Department that regulates the thrift industry, including all federal and state-chartered institutions that have federal deposit insurance.

off-record title defect A defect in title to real property that is not apparent from an examination of public records.

off-site costs Developers' costs for sewers, streets, and utilities incurred in the development of raw land but not connected with the actual construction, or on-site costs, of the building.

off-site management Property management functions that can be performed away from the premises being managed, such as accounting for rents collected and paying bills.

off-street parking Parking spaces located on private property, usually on an area provided especially for such use.

oil and gas lease A grant of the sole and exclusive right to extract oil and/or gas from beneath the surface of land.

on-frame modular A combination of modular construction constructed on nonremoveable steel frames. Generally, these are not built to HUD code (red label).

on or before A phrase in a contract referring to the time for performance of a specified act.

on-site improvement The construction of a building or other improvement within the boundaries of a property, thus increasing the property's value.

on-site management Those property-management functions that must be performed on the premises being managed, such as showing rental units, making repairs, and handling evictions.

open and notorious possession Possession sufficiently clear that a reasonable person viewing the property would know that the occupant claimed some title or interest in it.

open-end mortgage An expandable loan in which the borrower is given a limit up to which he or she may borrow, with each incremental advance to be secured by the same mortgage.

open house The common real estate practice of showing listed homes to the public during established hours.

open housing Housing offered on the market without any discrimination based on race, sex, color, handicap, familial status, religion, or national origin.

open listing A listing given to any number of brokers who can work simultaneously to sell the owner's property; the first broker to secure a buyer who is ready, willing, and able to purchase at the terms of the listing earns the commission.

open space
1. A certain portion of the landscape that has not been built upon and that is sought either

to be reserved in its natural state or used for agricultural or recreational purposes, such as parks, squares, and the like.

2. Park land within a subdivision, usually designated as such by a developer as a condition for receiving a building permit from the city or county.

open space act A tax law designed to encourage the preservation of qualified lands.

operating budget An itemized statement of income, expenses, net operating income before debt service, and cash flow.

operating expense ratio The ratio of operating expenses to potential gross income.

operating expenses Those recurring expenses essential to the continuous operation and maintenance of a property.

operation of law A term that describes the way in which rights and (sometimes) duties belong to a person by the mere application to a particular transaction of established rules of law, without any act by the person.

opinion of title An opinion by a person competent in examining titles as to the status of the record title of a property; not a guarantee of title.

option An agreement to keep open, for a set period, an offer to sell or lease real property.

option to renew A lease provision giving the tenant the right to extend the lease for an additional period of time on set terms.

oral contract A verbal contract.

ordinances The rules, regulations, and codes enacted into law by local governing bodies, which generally enact ordinances regulating such things as building standards, motor vehicle standards, and subdivision requirements.

ordinary and necessary business expense An expense incurred in the normal course of business, such as rent or expenditures for supplies, as opposed to expenses for a specific project or venture.

ordinary gain A gain or profit for which income tax must be paid at ordinary income rates.

oriented strandboard (OSB) A building material manufactured from waterproof, heat-cured adhesives and rectangular wood strands layered at right angles, similar to plywood.

origination fee The finance fee charged by a lender for making a mortgage.

ostensible agency An actual agency relationship that arises by the actions of the parties rather than by express agreement.

outparcel A tract of land adjacent to a larger tract of which it was originally an integral part.

O

outside of closing The payment of certain closing costs to someone directly, and not through the closing process, as reflected by the notation *POC* on the settlement statement.

outstanding balance The amount of a loan that remains to be paid.

overall rate (OAR) The direct percentage ratio between net annual operating income and sales price derived by dividing the net income by the price.

overflow right The temporary or permanent right to flood another person's land.

overhang The part of a roof that extends beyond the exterior wall.

overimprovement An improvement that by reason of its excessive cost is not the highest and best use of the site on which it is placed.

override
1. A provision in a listing agreement that protects a broker's right to a commission for a reasonable time after the agreement expires if the owner sells the property to a prospect with whom the broker negotiated during the time the listing was in effect.
2. A commission that is paid to managerial personnel, such as principal brokers, on sales made by the managers' subordinates.

overriding royalty A royalty fee retained by a lessee of an oil and gas lease when the property is subleased.

owner/occupant Property owner who physically occupies the property; the opposite of an absentee landlord or owner.

owner of record The person who appears in the public record as the owner of a particular property or mortgage.

owner's policy A title insurance policy, the proceeds of which are payable to the property owner; usually less extensive than the lender's policy.

P

package mortgage A method of financing in which the loan that finances the purchase of a home is also secured by personal items such as specified appliances.

pad

1. The area in a landlease park allocated for the placement of a manufactured home.
2. A foundation or site particularly suited for a specific type of improvement, such as a convenience store pad.

paired sales analysis A procedure used in the direct-sales comparison approach in which property sales are paired by similar property characteristics.

panelized construction Buildings constructed on-site with prebuilt factory products delivered to a construction site, where they are assembled into one housing unit.

panic peddling The illegal practice of soliciting sales or rental listings by making written or oral statements that create fear or alarm, transmit written or oral warnings or threats, solicit prospective renters or buyers of a protected class, or act in any other manner to induce or attempt to induce the sale or lease of residential property.

paper A business term referring to a mortgage, note, or contract for deed, which is usually taken back from the buyer by a seller when real property is sold.

par Average; equal, face value.

paragraph 17 The mortgage provision most frequently encountered that contains a due-on-sale clause; paragraph 17 of the Fannie Mae/Freddie Mac Uniform Instrument.

parcel A specific portion of a larger tract; a lot.

parity clause A provision that allows for a mortgage or trust deed to secure more than one note, and that provides that all notes be secured by the same mortgage without any priority or preference.

parol evidence rule A rule of evidence designed to achieve a degree of certainty in a transaction and to prevent fraudulent and perjured claims; a written contract prevails, and evidence of a prior oral agreement is generally inadmissible.

partial eviction A situation in which the landlord's negligence renders part of the premises unusable to the tenant for the purposes intended in the lease.

partially amortized A loan repayment schedule wherein payments on principal are insufficient to amortize the loan over its term; at maturity the remaining principal balance is due in full.

partially disclosed principal A situation in which a party to a transaction (such as a seller) knows, or has reason to know, that the agent to the transaction is working on behalf of a principal, but the seller is unable to discern the principal's identity.

partial reconveyance An instrument filed when a certain portion of encumbered real property is released from a mortgage or trust deed lien.

partial release clause A mortgage provision under which the mortgagee agrees to release certain parcels from the lien of the blanket mortgage upon payment by the mortgagor of a certain sum of money; frequently found in tract development construction loans.

partial taking In condemnation, the taking of only part of a privately owned property for public use.

participating broker A brokerage company or its sales agent who obtains a buyer for a property that is listed with another brokerage company, often called a *cooperating broker.*

participation certificate (PC) A mortgage-backed security sold by Freddie Mac to fund its purchases of mortgages and represent ownership interest in pools of mortgages purchased by Freddie Mac and serviced by the sellers.

participation mortgage
1. A mortgage in which the lender participates in the income of the mortgaged property beyond a fixed return, or receives a yield on the loan in addition to the straight interest rate.
2. A loan in which several lenders fund the loan.

parties The principals in a transaction or judicial proceeding.

partition
1. An interior wall.
2. The dividing of cotenants' interests in real property.

partnership An association of two or more persons who carry on a business for profit as co-owners as defined in the Uniform Partnership Act, in force in a majority of states.

party driveway A driveway located on both sides of a property line and used in common by the owners of each abutting property.

party to be charged The person referred to in the statute of frauds as the one against whom the contract is sought to be enforced; the one to be bound or held to the contract.

party wall A wall that is located on or at a boundary line between two adjoining parcels and is intended to be used by the owners of both properties in the construction or maintenance of improvements on their respective lots.

passive investor An investor who invests only capital and does not take an active role in the packaging, building, or managing of a project.

passive loss Loss from a passive activity, any activity that involves the conduct of any trade or business in which the taxpayer does not materially participate, and any rental activity.

pass-through The tax advantage of a partnership, limited liability company, or S corporation that permits income, profits, losses, and deductions to "pass through" the legal structure of the partnership directly to the individual investors who then pay any taxes due.

pass-through security A security issued by Ginnie Mae to mortgage investors.

payee The person to whom a debt instrument, such as a check or promissory note, is made payable; the obligee; the receiver.

payment bond A surety bond by which a contractor assures an owner that material and labor furnished in the construction of a building will be fully paid for, and that no mechanics' liens will be filed.

P

payoff The payment in full of an existing loan, usually at the time of refinancing or upon the sale or transfer of a secured property.

payor The party who makes payment to another.

penalty A punishment imposed for violating a law or an agreement.

pension fund
1. An institution holding assets invested in long-term mortgages and high-grade stocks and bonds to accumulate funds with which to provide individuals with retirement income according to a prearranged plan; often a source for real estate financing.
2. A pension or profit-sharing plan.

percentage lease A lease whose rental is based on a percentage of the monthly or annual gross sales made on the premises, common with large retail stores, especially in shopping centers.

percolation test A hydraulic engineer's test of soil to determine the ability of the ground to absorb and drain water; also called a **perk test.**

perfect escrow An escrow in which all the documents, funds, and instructions needed to close the transaction are in the hands of the escrow agent.

perfecting title The process of eliminating any claims against a title, such as having a wife execute a quitclaim deed to release any possible dower claim.

P

performance bond A bond, usually posted by one who is to perform work for another, ensuring that a project or undertaking will be completed as per agreement or contract.

periodic costs The fixed property expenses (like taxes and insurance) that occur on a regular but infrequent basis.

periodic tenancy A leasehold estate that continues from period to period; all conditions and terms of the tenancy continue for an uncertain time until proper notice of termination is given.

permanent financing A long-term loan, as opposed to an interim short-term loan.

permissive waste The failure of lessees or life tenants to maintain and make reasonable repairs to the real property under their control.

person A legal person is not always necessarily an individual but may also be a corporation, a government or governmental agency, a business trust, an estate, a trust, an association, a partnership, a joint venture, two or more persons having a joint or common interest, or any other legal or commercial entity.

personal assistant A person who works for another licensed real estate agent who employs the assistant to perform tasks such as handling paperwork, setting up appointments, coordinating marketing efforts, and so on.

personal liability The obligation to satisfy a debt to the extent of one's personal assets.

P

personal property Tangible and movable property, such as chattels (also called personalty).

personal representative The title given to the person designated in a will or appointed by the probate court to settle the estate of a deceased person.

per-unit cost method A method of computing a property management fee based on the direct cost of managing a specific number of rental units.

petition A formal request or application to an authority, such as a court, seeking specific relief or redress of some wrong.

Phase I audit An initial evaluation of a property site to determine potential contamination or non-compliance with environmental laws and regulations, often required by lenders for commercial and industrial properties.

physical deterioration A reduction in utility or value resulting from an impairment of physical condition, which can be divided into either curable or incurable types of deterioration.

physical life The actual age or life span over which a structure is considered habitable, as opposed to its economic life.

piggyback loan A type of financing that seeks to avoid private mortgage insurance (PMI) utilizing a first mortgage at 80 percent of value and a second (or third) mortgage "piggybacked" onto the first loan.

PITI Abbreviation for principal, interest, taxes, and insurance, originally found in an all-inclusive mortgage payment, but may also include private mortgage insurance (PMI), mortgage insurance premiums (MIP), flood insurance, and home-owner association dues.

placement fee A fee charged by a mortgage broker for negotiating a loan between a lender and borrower.

plain language law A federal or state law that requires certain consumer contracts to be written in a clear and coherent manner, using words with common everyday meanings and appropriately divided and captioned by its various sections.

plaintiff A person who brings a lawsuit; the complainant.

planned unit development (PUD) A nontraditional type of housing development designed to produce a high density of dwellings, maximum use of open spaces, and greater flexibility for residential land and development; local government approval is required. The developer records a declaration of covenants and restrictions and records a subdivision plat reserving common areas to the members of the association but *not* to the general public and a nonprofit community association is organized to provide for maintenance of the common areas.

planning commission An official agency usually organized on the city, county, or regional level to develop a master plan and control the use, design, and development of land.

plans and specifications All the drawings pertaining to a development under consideration and the written instructions to the builder pertaining to the details appearing on the working drawings.

plat book A public record of maps of subdivided land showing the division of the land into blocks, lots, and parcels, and indicating the dimensions of individual parcels.

plat map A map of a town, section, or subdivision indicating the location and boundaries of individual properties.

pledge The transfer or delivery of property to a lender to be held as security for repayment of a debt.

plot plan A plan showing the layout of improvements on a property site; a plot.

plottage value The increased usability and value resulting from the combining or consolidating of adjacent lots into one larger lot.

pocket license card Evidence of real estate licensure, sometimes called a "wallet card," issued by the state real estate licensing agency.

pocket listing A listing that is retained by the listing broker or salesperson, and is not made available to other brokers in the office or to other multiple listing service members; strongly discouraged by the profession and forbidden by many multiple listing services.

point of beginning (POB) The starting point in a metes-and-bounds description of property; a legal description of a property must always return to the point of beginning to describe the area accurately.

points A generic term for a percentage of the principal conventional loan amount; a rate adjustment factor; each point is equal to 1 percent of the loan amount; a onetime charge paid for the use of money.

police power The constitutional authority and inherent power of a state to adopt and enforce laws and regulations to promote and support the public health, safety, morals, and general welfare.

portfolio loan A loan originated and maintained by the lending institution and not sold in the secondary mortgage market.

positive cash flow The number of dollars remaining after collecting rental income and paying operating expenses and mortgage payments.

possession The act of either actually or constructively possessing or occupying property.

possibility of reverter A possibility that property granted under a deed may revert back to the grantor if the grantee breaches a condition subject to which the property was granted.

postdated check A check that on its face is dated later than the actual date of signing and therefore is not negotiable until the later date arrives, because a bank cannot make payment before the stated date; considered valid, unless it was postdated for an illegal purpose.

P

potable water Water that can be safely and agreeably used for drinking.

power of attorney A written instrument authorizing a person, the attorney-in-fact, to act as the agent on behalf of another to the extent indicated in the instrument.

power of sale A clause in a mortgage authorizing the holder of the mortgage to sell the property at public auction without a judicial action in the event of the borrower's default; the proceeds from the public sale are used to pay off the mortgage debt first, and any surplus is paid to the mortgagor.

practice of law Rendering services that are peculiar to the law profession, such as preparing legal documents, giving legal advice and counsel, or construing contracts by which legal rights are secured.

preapproved loan A pending loan in which all of the underlying documents are in file and there is a strong probability that there are no credit or income issues that will stop the loan from closing; it does not necessarily mean that the file has been underwritten by the lender who will commit to provide the funds for closing.

P

preclosing A preliminary meeting preceding the formal closing where documents are prepared, reviewed, and signed, and where estimated prorations are made well in advance of the closing date.

predatory lending A variety of unscrupulous lending practices by the lender to make loans secured by a home or car with the intention that the borrower will be unable to repay the loan, thus allowing the lender to repossess the home or car to resell at a profit.

preemption
1. A clause sometimes inserted in a deed of subdivided land, in which the developer either retains the right of first refusal upon resale of the property or relinquishes that right to the owner of an adjacent lot who may exercise the right when the property is offered for sale.
2. A legal doctrine in which one law is superior to another.

preliminary costs Those costs incurred in conjunction with, but prior to, actual commencement of the main project.

preliminary report A title report that is made before a title insurance policy is issued or when escrow is opened; not a binder or commitment that the title company will thereafter insure the title to the property.

premises
1. A specific section of a deed that states the names of the parties, the recital of consideration, and the legal description of the property.
2. The subject property, such as the property that is deeded or the unit that is leased.

P

premium
1. The consideration given to invite a loan or a bargain, such as the consideration paid to the assignor by the assignee of a lease or a contract such as an option.
2. The amount paid for insurance coverage.

prepaid expenses Expenses that are paid before they are currently due, also called prepaids.

prepaid interest The paying of interest before it is due.

prepaid items A lump-sum payment to establish a reserve or impound account.

prepayment Early payment of a debt.

prepayment penalty The amount set by the creditor as a penalty to the debtor for paying off the debt before it matures; an early-withdrawal charge.

prepayment privilege The right of the debtor to pay off part or all of a debt, without penalty or premium or other fee, prior to maturity, such as in a mortgage or agreement of sale.

prequalified loan A pending loan in which a loan officer opines that, based on a preliminary interview and a credit report, the borrower will be able to meet the loan requirements, assuming the borrower is telling the truth about his or her financial situation and income status.

presale A prior-to-construction sales program by a developer.

prescription Acquiring a right in property, usually in the form of an intangible property right such as an easement or right-of-way, by means of adverse use of property that is continuous and uninterrupted for the prescriptive period established by state statute.

present value of one dollar A doctrine based on the fact that money has a time value; the present worth of a payment to be received at some time in the future is the amount which, at a given fixed interest rate, will grow to the amount of the payment over the projected term.

preservation district A zoning district established to protect and preserve parkland, wilderness areas, open spaces, beach reserves, scenic areas, historic sites, open ranges, watersheds, water supplies, fish, and wildlife, and to promote forestry and grazing.

presumption A rule of law that provides that a court will draw a particular inference from a certain fact or evidence unless and until the truth of such inference is disproved or rebutted.

prevailing party The person who wins a lawsuit.

prevailing rate A general term to describe the average interest rate currently being charged by banks and lending institutions on mortgage loans.

price The quantity of one thing exchanged for another; the amount of money paid for an item; the consideration; the purchase price.

price fixing The illegal practice of conspiring to establish fixed fees or prices for services rendered or goods sold; a violation of antitrust laws.

prima facie evidence A legal term used to refer to evidence that is good and sufficient on its face ("at first view") to establish a given fact or prove a case; presumptive evidence.

primary mortgage market The market in which lenders originate loans and make funds available directly to borrowers, bear the risk of long-term financing, and usually service the loan until the debt is discharged.

prime rate The minimum interest rate charged by a commercial bank on short-term loans to its largest and strongest clients (those with the highest credit standings); often used as a base rate for other business and personal loans.

prime tenant A tenant (or related group of tenants) who is the largest single occupant of a building.

principal
1. One of the main parties to a transaction.
2. In a fiduciary relationship, the person who hires a real estate broker to represent him or her in the sale of property.
3. The capital sum on which interest is paid.

principal broker (PB) Under some state license laws, the licensed broker directly in charge of and responsible for the real estate operations conducted by a brokerage company.

principal meridian The prime meridian intersecting the reference marker of a survey that is used as a reference line for numbering ranges.

principal residence A structure actually and physically occupied by the taxpayer.

principles of appraisal The theories and economic concepts that explain the rationale of market behavior affecting value, including the theories of anticipation, change, competition, balance, substitution, supply, and demand.

prior appropriation A theory of water law based on the principle, restated as "first in time is first in right," that regards the right to divert water from a water source.

priority The order of position, time, or place.

private mortgage insurance (PMI) A special form of insurance designed to permit lenders to increase their loan-to-market-value ratio, often up to 97 percent of the market value of the property; typically insures the top 20 to 25 percent of the loan.

private offering An offering of a real estate security that is exempt from registration with state and/or federal regulatory agencies because it does not involve a public offering; it is still subject to the full disclosure and antifraud provisions of the securities laws.

P

probate The formal judicial proceeding to prove or confirm the validity of a will, to collect the assets of the decedent's estate, to pay the debts and taxes, and to determine the persons to whom the remainder of the estate is to pass.

proceed order A written order to a general contractor to proceed with a change in contract requirements, subject to a later equitable adjustment of the contract price and/or completion time as specified in the contract.

proceeds-of-loan escrow An escrow in which loan proceeds are deposited by the lender pending the closing of a real estate transaction.

procuring cause That effort that brings about the desired result.

profit and loss statement A detailed statement of the income and expenses of a business that reveals the operating position of the business over a certain time.

profit a prendre A right to take part of the soil and produce of the land, such as the right to take coal, fruit, or timber.

pro forma In form only; not necessarily official.

pro forma statement A projection of future income and expenses or other results.

progression A principle of appraisal, which states that the worth of a lesser object is increased by being located among better objects; the opposite of regression.

progress payments Payments of money scheduled in relation to the completion of portions of a construction project.

promissory note An unconditional written promise of one person to pay a certain sum of money to another, or order, or bearer, at a future specified time.

promulgate To publish; to print.

property The rights or interests a person has in the thing he or she owns but not, technically, the thing itself; called the *bundle of rights,* including the right to possess, to use, to encumber, to transfer, and to exclude. In modern understanding, however, property has come to mean the thing itself to which certain ownership rights are attached, either real or personal.

property management That aspect of the real estate profession devoted to the leasing, managing, marketing, and overall maintenance of the property of others.

property report A disclosure document required under the federal Interstate Land Sales Full Disclosure Act where applicable to the interstate sale of subdivided lots.

property residual technique An appraisal technique similar to the building residual technique and the land residual technique of capitalization, except that the net income is considered attributable to the total real property.

property tax A tax levied by the government against property; real property is often taxed due to its immobility and consequent ease to locate, evaluate, and tax. Only state and local governments may tax real property.

proposition The instrument used to submit an offer; similar to proposed offer to purchase in some states.

proprietary lease A written lease in a cooperative apartment building, between the owner/corporation and the tenant/stockholder, in which the tenant is given the right to occupy a particular unit; differs from the typical landlord-tenant lease in that the tenant is also a stockholder in the corporation that owns the building.

proprietorship Ownership of a business or income property.

prorate To divide or distribute proportionately.

prospect A party who may be interested in buying or selling real property.

prospectus A printed statement distributed to describe and give advance information on a business, venture, project, or stock issue.

protected class Any group of people designated as such by the Department of Housing and Urban Development (HUD) in consideration of federal and state civil rights legislation; currently includes race, color, religion, national origin, sex, familial status, handicap, and other groups.

P

proxy A person temporarily authorized to act or do business on behalf of another; also refers to the document giving such person the power to act for another—a power of attorney.

public land Land owned by the federal government and available for purchase by a private citizen when the land is no longer needed for government purposes.

public offering statement The document prepared by a subdivider in accordance with individual state subdivision laws requiring disclosure of all material facts about a subdivision to be offered for sale to the public.

public sale An auction sale for the public, which has been informed by notice or by invitation so as to have the opportunity to engage in competitive bidding at a place to which the public has access.

puffing Exaggerated or superlative comments or opinions not made as representations of fact and thus not grounds for misrepresentation.

punch list A discrepancy list showing defects in construction that need some corrective work to bring the building up to standards set by the plans and specifications.

P

punitive damages Exemplary or vindictive court-awarded damages to an injured party, the purpose of which is to punish the perpetrator, not to reward the injured party.

pur autre vie A life estate pur autre vie is a life estate that is measured by the life of a person other than the grantee.

purchase-money mortgage (PMM) A mortgage given as part of the buyer's consideration for the purchase of real property, and delivered at the same time that the real property is transferred as a simultaneous part of the transaction; commonly a mortgage taken back by a seller from a purchaser in lieu of purchase money.

purchaser's policy A title insurance policy, also called an owner's policy, generally furnished by a seller to a purchaser under a real estate sales contract or contract for deed, insuring the property against defect in record title.

pyramiding A process of acquiring additional properties through refinancing properties already owned and then reinvesting the loan proceeds in additional property.

Q

quadraplex (quad) A four-unit residential building designed to provide each unit with privacy and a separate entrance.

qualification The process of reviewing a prospective borrower's credit and payment capacity before approving a loan.

qualified acceptance An acceptance, in law, that amounts to a rejection of an offer and is a counteroffer; an acceptance of an offer upon certain named conditions, or one that has the effect of altering or modifying the terms of the offer.

qualified buyer A buyer who has demonstrated the financial capacity and creditworthiness required to afford the offered price.

qualified fee An estate in fee that is subject to certain limitations imposed by the owner.

qualified intermediary The individual or company (disinterested third party) who acts as the facilitator of a 1031 exchange.

quantity survey A method of estimating construction cost or reproduction cost; a highly technical process used in arriving at the cost estimate of new construction and sometimes referred to in the building trade as the *price takeoff method.*

quarter-section A land-area measure used in connection with the government (rectangular) survey of land measurement; a quarter-section of land is 160 acres.

quash To annul or to set aside, as in quashing a summons or an administrative complaint.

quasi Latin for "as if"; similar to; almost like. Commonly used in real estate with such terms as *quasi contract, quasi-judicial,* and *quasi corporation.*

Q

quick assets Assets that are quickly and easily convertible into cash; liquid assets.

quiet enjoyment The right of an owner or lessee legally in possession of property to uninterrupted use of the property without interference from the former owner, lessor, or any third party claiming superior title.

quiet title action A court action intended to establish or settle the title to a particular property, especially where there is a cloud on the title, often used to extinguish easements; remove any clouds on title; release a homestead, dower, or curtesy interest; transfer title without warranties; clear tax titles; or simply release an interest when the grantor may have some remote claim to the property.

quitclaim deed A deed of conveyance that operates, in effect, as a release of whatever interest the grantor has in the property; sometimes called a *release deed;* grantors do not warrant title or possession.

quorum The minimum legal number of people required to be present before a specified meeting can officially take place or authorized business can be transacted.

R

radon A colorless, odorless, naturally occurring gas produced from the decay of natural radioactive minerals in the ground found in buildings in every state and territory; the EPA suggested action level is four.

range
1. An open land area for grazing.
2. A series of mountains.

range line A measurement, used in the government survey system, consisting of a strip of land six miles wide, running in a north-south direction. (See **government survey method, township**)

range of value The market value of a property; usually stated as a variable amount between a low and a high limit.

rate of return The relationship (expressed as a percentage) between the annual net income that is generated by a business and the invested capital (or the appraised value or the gross income) of the business.

ratification The adoption or confirmation of an act already performed on behalf of a person without prior authorization.

raw land Unimproved land; land in its unused, natural state before grading, construction, subdividing, or improvements such as streets, lighting, and sewers.

"ready, willing, and able" A phrase referring to a prospective buyer of property who is legally capable, willing, and financially able to consummate the transaction.

R

real estate The physical land at, above, and below the earth's surface including all appurtenances, i.e., any structures.

real estate agent A term commonly used to refer to a licensed salesperson working for a licensed broker, even if the salesperson has already obtained his or her individual broker's license.

real estate commission/department A state governmental agency whose primary duties include making rules and regulations to protect the general public involved in real estate transactions, granting licenses to real estate brokers and salespeople, and suspending or revoking licenses for cause.

real estate education, research, and recovery fund A special state fund, in some states, supported either by a portion of the real estate licensing fees or by a special fee, used to encourage real estate education and to provide a source of financial relief for persons injured by the fraudulent practices of a judgment-proof licensee.

real estate investment trust (REIT) A method of pooling investment money from at least 100 investors, providing favored tax treatment for certain business trusts by exempting from corporate tax certain qualified REITs that invest at least 75 percent of their assets in real estate and that distribute 95 percent or more of their annual real estate ordinary income to their investors; REIT shares sell like stock on the major exchanges investing in real estate directly, either through properties or mortgages.

real estate mortgage investment conduit (REMIC) A special tax vehicle for entities that issue multiple classes in investor interests backed by a pool of mortgages.

real estate mortgage trust (REMT) A type of REIT that buys and sells real estate mortgages (usually short-term junior instruments) rather than real property.

real estate owned (REO) A term used by lenders to describe real property involuntarily acquired by them through foreclosure.

Real Estate Settlement Procedures Act (RESPA) A federal law that ensures that the buyer and seller in a real estate transaction receive information of all settlement costs when the purchase of a one-to-four family residential dwelling is financed by a federally related mortgage loan; such information includes the special information booklet, good-faith estimate of settlement costs, use of the standardized Uniform Settlement Statement, and prohibition against kickbacks.

realized gain The profit made on the sale of a capital asset; usually the difference between the net sales price (amount realized) and the adjusted tax basis of the property.

real property The earth's surface, the air above, and the ground below, as well as all appurtenances to the land including buildings, structures,

R

fixtures, fences, and improvements erected upon or affixed to the same, excluding growing crops, and the interests, benefits, and rights inherent in the ownership of real estate (the bundle of rights).

real property securities registration The process of disclosure and notification to proper government agencies of an issuer's intended real property security offering.

realty Land and everything permanently affixed thereto; the opposite of personalty.

reappraisal lease A lease that provides for periodic reevaluation of property, with the rent set as a percentage of the appraised value.

reasonable time A fair length of time that may be allowed or required for an act to be completed, considering the nature of the act and the surrounding circumstances.

rebate A reduction of a stipulated charge.

recapture To tax at the same rate as the previous deduction, i.e., ordinary tax.

recapture clause A clause usually found in percentage leases, especially in shopping center leases, giving the landlord the right to terminate the lease, and thus recapture the premises, if the tenant does not maintain a specified minimum amount of business.

recapture rate An appraisal term describing that rate at which invested capital will be returned over the period of time a prudent investor would

R

expect to recapture his or her investment in a wasting asset.

recasting The process of redesigning existing loans, especially where there is a default.

receipt A written acknowledgment of having received something.

receiver An independent party appointed by a court to impartially receive, preserve, and manage property that is involved in litigation, pending final disposition of the matter before the court.

reciprocal easements Easements typically arising upon the development of a planned subdivision, in which easements and restrictions are created as covenants limiting the use of the land for the benefit of all the owners in the entire tract.

reciprocity The practice of mutual exchanges of privileges.

recital of consideration A statement of what constitutes the consideration for a particular transaction.

reclamation The process of converting wasted natural resources into productive assets, such as desert land reclaimed through irrigation or swampland that is filled in.

recognition A precise tax term meaning that the transaction is a taxable event; if a gain or loss is "recognized," the gain is taxable and the loss is deductible.

R

recognition clause A clause found in some blanket mortgages and contracts for deed used to purchase a tract of land for subdivision and development providing for protection of the rights of the ultimate buyers of individual lots in case of default under the blanket mortgage by the developer.

reconciliation
1. The final step in an appraisal process, in which the appraiser brings together the estimates of value received from the direct sales comparison, cost, and income approaches to arrive at a final estimate of value for the subject property.
2. The balancing of entries in a double-entry accounting system.

reconveyance The act of conveying title in property back to the original owner.

recording The act of entering into the book of public records the written instruments affecting the title to real property, such as deeds, mortgages, contracts for sale, options, and assignments; failure to record a document does not impair its validity as between the parties thereto and all other parties having notice of its existence.

record owner The owner of property as shown by an examination of the records; the one having record title.

R

record title Title as it appears from an examination of the public records.

recourse note A debt instrument with which the lender can take action against the borrower or endorser personally in addition to foreclosure of the property covering the lender's mortgage.

recovery fund A state-regulated fund generally defined and described in the state real estate license law used as a source of money to indemnify buyers and sellers of real estate who have suffered losses due to a real estate licensee's misrepresentation or fraudulent acts (usually not negligent acts).

recreational lease A contract in which the lessor (usually a developer) leases recreationally related facilities (tennis courts, gyms, swimming pools) to a tenant for a stipulated time and rent consideration.

reddendum clause A clause in a conveyance that reserves something for the grantor, such as rent payable to a lessor or an interest in a life estate to a remainderman.

redemption, equitable right of The right of a mortgagor who has defaulted on the mortgage note to redeem or get back his or her title to the property by paying off the entire mortgage note before the foreclosure sale; the right comes into existence immediately upon execution of the mortgage and continues to exist until the mortgage is satisfied and discharged by payment or

R

until the right of redemption is cut off by foreclosure sale.

redemption period A period of time established by state law during which a property owner has a right to redeem real estate after a foreclosure or tax sale by paying the sales price, interest, and costs, available in some states.

redevelopment The improvement of cleared or undeveloped land, usually in an urban renewal area.

redevelopment agency A quasi-governmental agency whose primary purposes are to develop property or improve housing opportunities in urban renewal areas and to relocate residents displaced by the redevelopment of the area.

red flag A condition that warns a reasonably observant person of a potential problem, thus suggesting further investigation.

red herring A preliminary prospectus for the sale of a security filed with the Securities and Exchange Commission but the registration of which has not yet become effective.

rediscount rate The rate of interest charged by the Federal Reserve Bank for loans to member banks; also called the **discount rate.**

redlining A practice by some lending institutions that restricts the number of loans or the loan-to-value ratio in certain areas of a community because of a class of risk such as racial composition, or because it is a low-income

R

neighborhood, rather than distinguishing among individual risks.

reduction certificate An instrument that shows the current amount of the unpaid balance of a mortgage, the rate of interest, and the date of maturity.

reentry The repossession of real property in accordance with a legal right reserved when the original possession was transferred; to be distinguished from the right of entry that a landlord possesses to go in and inspect the leased premises.

referee A disinterested, neutral party appointed by a court to arbitrate, investigate, find facts, or settle some dispute or legal matter.

referral The act of recommending or referring; a sales lead.

referral agency
1. A licensed brokerage company in which licensed salespeople agree to perform no other brokerage service but to obtain leads on prospective buyers and sellers.
2. A brokerage company participating in a national or regional network of relocation services.

refinance To obtain a new loan to pay off an existing loan; to pay off one loan with the proceeds from another.

reformation A legal action necessary to correct or modify a contract or deed that has not accurately

R

reflected the intentions of the parties, due to some mechanical error, such as a typographical error in the legal description.

regional shopping center A large shopping center containing from 70 to 225 stores and more than 400,000 square feet of leasable area.

registered land Land registered in the Torrens system.

registrar (recorder) The person usually having the duty to maintain accurate official records of all deeds, mortgages, contracts for deed, and other instruments relating to real estate titles filed for recordation; often associated with the Torrens system of title registration.

regression A principle of appraisal stating that, between dissimilar properties, the worth of the better property is adversely affected by the presence of the lesser-quality property.

regular system (REG) A system of recordation of documents affecting land not registered in the Torrens system; also known as the *unregistered system*.

regulation A rule or order prescribed for management or government, as in the rules and regulations of the real estate commission that generally have the force and effect of law once the commission's regulations are approved by the governor following a public hearing.

Regulation A A special exemption from standard SEC registration of a security issue where the aggregate amount of the offering is less than $1.5 million.

Regulation B A Federal Reserve System regulation covering the Equal Credit Opportunity Act.

Regulation D An SEC regulation containing a set of rules exempting from registration certain limited security offerings.

Regulation T A federal regulation, administered by the Federal Reserve Board, governing the extension of credit arrangements for the extension of credit by securities brokers and dealers.

Regulation Z Implements the Truth-in-Lending Act.

rehabilitate (rehab) To restore to a former or improved condition, such as when buildings are renovated and modernized.

reinstatement To bring something back to its prior position, as in restoring a lapsed insurance policy or restoring a defaulted loan to paid-up status.

reinsurance A contract by which the original insurer (the ceding company) obtains insurance from another insurer (the reinsuring company) against loss on the ceding company's original policy.

reissue rate A reduced charge by a title insurance company for a new policy if a previous policy on the same property was recently issued.

related parties Parties standing in a certain defined relationship to each other; parties may be

R

related by blood, by fiduciary relationships, or by ownership interest in a corporation.

relation-back doctrine A doctrine establishing the effects of the grantor's death on an escrow transaction; death of the grantor does not terminate the escrow or revoke the agent's authority to deliver an executed deed.

release The discharge or relinquishment of a right, claim, or privilege.

release clause
1. A provision found in many blanket mortgages enabling the mortgagor to obtain partial releases of specific parcels from the mortgage upon a payment larger than the pro rata portion of the loan.
2. A contingency provision in a purchase agreement, which allows the seller to continue to market the property and accept other offers.

reliction The gradual recession of water from the usual watermark and, therefore, an increase of the land; the new land usually belongs to the riparian owner.

relinquished property The first property transferred in a delayed tax-deferred exchange; the up-leg property.

relocation clause A lease provision giving the landlord the right to relocate a tenant.

relocation company A company retained by large corporations to help their employees move from one location to another.

remainder estate A future interest in real estate created at the same time and by the same instrument as another estate, and limited to arise immediately upon the termination of the prior estate; a future estate created by the grantor in favor of some third party.

remainderman One entitled to take an estate in remainder.

remediation
1. The process of remedying or curing a condition, such as sealing or removing lead-based paint or installing a radon mitigation system.
2. The process of implementing a plan to clean up a site identified as containing hazardous substances.

remise To give up; to remit; typical language found in a quitclaim deed.

renegotiable rate mortgage (RRM) A short-term loan secured by a long-term adjustable rate mortgage, with interest renegotiated at the time of established automatic renewal periods.

renegotiation of lease The review of an existing lease after a specified period of time to negotiate the lease terms anew, most often to establish a new annual rent for an additional period based on changed economic conditions.

renewal option A lease covenant that gives the lessee the right to extend the lease term for a certain period, on specified terms, provided the tenant is not in default.

R

rent Fixed periodic payment made by a tenant or occupant of property to the owner for the possession and use, usually by prior agreement of the parties, usually paid in advance.

rentable area The area computed by measuring to the inside finish of permanent outer building walls, to the office side of corridors and/or permanent partitions, and to the center of partitions that separate the premises from adjoining rentable areas; no deductions are made for columns and projections necessary to the buildings.

rental agent (leasing agent) Any person who for compensation or other valuable consideration acts or attempts to act as an intermediary between a person seeking to lease, sublease, or assign a housing accommodation and a person seeking to acquire a lease, sublease, or assignment of a housing accommodation.

rental agreement A written or oral agreement that establishes or modifies the terms, conditions, rules, regulations, or any other provisions concerning the use and occupancy of a dwelling unit and premises; a lease on residential property.

rental pool A rental arrangement whereby participating owners of rental apartments agree to have their units available for rental as determined by the rental agent, and then share in the profits and losses of all the rental apartments in the pool according to an agreed-on formula.

R

rent control Regulation by state or local governmental agencies restricting the amount of rent or the rental increase; such regulation has been upheld as a valid exercise of the state's police power in the jurisdictions that currently employ rent controls.

rent escalation Adjustment of rent by the lessor to reflect changes in cost of living or property maintenance costs.

rent roll A list of tenants showing the unit occupied and the rent paid by each.

rent-up The process of filling a new building with tenants.

repairs Current expenditures to restore to an original condition; minor alterations made to maintain the property rather than to extend the useful life of the property.

replacement cost The cost of constructing a building with current materials and techniques that is identical in functional utility to the structure being appraised and that is designed in accordance with current materials, styles, and standards.

replacement property The property exchanged for in a tax-deferred exchange.

replevin Legal proceedings brought to recover possession of personal property unlawfully taken, as when a landlord has unlawfully taken the personal belongings of the tenant due to the tenant's failure to pay the rent.

R

reproduction cost   The current cost of building a replica of the subject structure, using the same materials and construction standards, the exact duplication.

rescind   To annul, cancel a contract. One may rescind a contract and revoke an offer. (See **rescission, revocation, revoke**)

rescission   The legal remedy of canceling, terminating, or annulling a contract and restoring the parties to their original positions; a return to the status quo, as a result of mistake, fraud, or misrepresentation; there is no need to show any money damage.

rescission clause
 1. A specific clause occasionally found in a contract for deed that requires the seller to return all of the buyer's payments, minus the cost and a fair rental value, if the buyer defaults.
 2. A clause in a contract, required by some state subdivided land sales laws, that informs a purchaser of his or her rescission rights as provided by state law.

reservation   The creation, on behalf of the grantor, of a new right issuing from what was granted.

reservation money   Money used as earnest money deposit to hold a property being offered for sale.

reserve for replacements   A typical entry in an operating statement to provide for the replacement of short-life items, such as air-conditioning units, carpeting, and appliances; an allowance that is necessary to maintain a projected level of income.

reserve fund Monies a lender will often require a borrower to set aside as a cushion of capital for future payment of items such as taxes, insurance, and deferred maintenance; an *impound account* or *customer's trust fund*.

residence One's home or place of abode.

residence property Raw land or improved property with buildings designed for human occupation, such as single-family homes or condominium units.

residence, sale of The Taxpayer Relief Act of 1997 provides the owner who has resided in the principal residence for two of the last five years, a capital gains tax exclusion of up to $500,000 for married taxpayers filing jointly and $250,000 for those filing singly.

resident manager A salaried agent of the owner employed to manage a single building.

residual
1. That which is left over, such as the residual value of property after its economic life is completed.
2. Deferred commissions; that is, commissions that are earned but payment of which is put off for a stated period.

R

residual process An appraisal process, used in the income approach, to estimate the value of the land and/or the building, as indicated by the capitalization of the residual net income attributable to it.

resort property Property that lends itself to vacationing, recreation, and/or leisure enjoyment because of its natural resources, beauty, or its improvements.

respondeat superior A principle of agency law that states that the employer (principal) is liable in certain cases for the wrongful acts of his or her employee (agent) committed during the course of employment, so long as those acts of the agent were performed within the scope of the agent's authority.

restraint of trade Contracts or combinations that are designed to eliminate or stifle competition, to create a monopoly, to control prices, or otherwise to hamper or obstruct the free operation of business; these actions are generally illegal under federal and state antitrust laws.

restraint on alienation A limitation or condition placed on the right to transfer property.

restriction A limitation on the use of property; private restrictions created by means of covenants, conditions, and restrictions (CC&Rs) written into real property instruments, such as deeds and leases, and usually enforced by means of court injunction.

R

restrictive covenant A private agreement usually contained in a deed or lease that restricts the use and occupancy of real property (sometimes called *private zoning*); it is said to *run with the land* and binds all subsequent purchasers, their heirs, and assigns.

resubdivision The act of taking an existing subdivision and either replatting it or dividing it even further.

retainage A portion or a percentage of payments withheld by the landowner or contractor until the construction contract has been satisfactorily completed, the period for filing mechanics' liens has expired, or when the lien has been released by the contractor and subcontractors.

retaining wall
1. Any wall erected to hold back or support a bank of earth.
2. Any enclosing wall built to resist the lateral pressure of internal loads.

retaliatory eviction An act whereby a landlord evicts a tenant in response to some complaint made by the tenant; however, after a complaint is made by the tenant, a landlord can still evict a tenant for good cause, such as nonpayment of rent or violation of the building rules.

reverse annuity mortgage (RAM) A form of mortgage that enables elderly homeowners to borrow against the equity in their homes so they can receive monthly payments needed to help

R

meet living costs; the loan comes due either upon a specific date or upon the occurrence of a specific event, such as sale of the property or death of the borrower.

reversion The estate remaining in the grantor, or the estate of a testator, who has conveyed a lesser estate from the original; a future estate in real property created by operation of law when a grantor conveys a lesser estate than he or she has.

reversionary factor A mathematical factor found in present worth tables used to convert a single, lump-sum future payment into present value, given the proper discount rate and time period.

reversionary value The expected worth of a property at the end of the anticipated holding period.

review appraiser An appraiser who analyzes the written reports of other appraisers to determine validity of the data and the conclusions; often working for a bank, insurance company, or the government.

revocation The act of terminating, canceling, or annulling an offer, as when a seller revokes a broker's agency by canceling the listing.

revoke The process of terminating, canceling, or annulling an offer.

rider An addition, amendment, or endorsement ("special endorsement") annexed to a document and incorporated into the terms of the document.

R

right of contribution The right of one who has discharged a common liability to recover from another liable party his or her pro rata share.

right of first refusal The right of a person to have the first opportunity to either purchase or lease real property; unlike an option, the holder of a right of first refusal has no right to purchase until the owner actually offers the property for sale or entertains an offer to purchase from some third party.

right of re-entry The future interest left in the transferor of property who transfers an estate on condition subsequent; the transferor must take affirmative steps to terminate the estate, such as file a suit in court; otherwise the condition may be discharged.

right of survivorship The distinctive characteristics of a joint tenancy (also tenancy by entirety) by which the surviving joint tenant(s) succeeds to all right, title, and interest of the deceased joint tenant without the need for probate proceedings.

right-of-way (R/W)
1. The right or privilege, acquired through accepted usage or by contract, to pass over a designated portion of the property of another.
2. Land either owned by a railroad or over which it maintains an easement for operating on its trackage in accordance with government safety regulations and industry standards.

R

right, title, and interest A term often used in conveyancing documents to describe the transfer of all that the grantor or assignor is capable of transferring.

right-to-use
1. The legal right to use or occupy a property.
2. A contractual right to occupy a time-share unit under a license, vacation lease, or club membership arrangement.

riparian lease An agreement covering the terms of leasing lands situated between the high-water mark and the low-water mark.

riparian rights Those rights and obligations that are incidental to ownership of land adjacent to or abutting on watercourses such as streams and lakes; riparian rights do not attach except where there is a water boundary on one side of the particular tract of land claimed to be riparian.

riser The vertical face of the step that supports the tread.

risk capital Capital invested in a speculative venture, thus being the least secure and offering the greatest chance of loss but often yielding the greatest rate of return.

risk factor The portion of a rate of return on an investment that is assumed to cover the risk associated with that investment; the greater the risk, the higher the capitalization rate.

R

risk of loss Responsibility for damages caused to improvements.

road A collector roadway in a rural district, generally without full improvements such as curbs and sidewalks.

rollover
1. Refers to tax provisions that enable the taxpayer to defer paying taxes in certain situations such as the exchange of real property or involuntary conversion.
2. In a financing sense, the practice of rewriting a new loan at the termination of a prior loan; a clause often found in adjustable-rate loans.

root title The conveyance or instrument that starts the chain of land title; the original source of title.

row house One of a series of individual homes having architectural unity and a common wall between units and the land in front of, under, and behind the house is individually owned.

royalty
1. The money paid to an owner of realty for the right of depleting the property of its natural resources, such as oil, gas, minerals, stone, builders' sand and gravel, and timber.
2. A franchise fee.

rule against perpetuities A rule of law designed to require the early vesting of a future contingent interest in real property and thus prevent the

R

property from being made inalienable for long periods of time.

run with the land A phrase describing rights or covenants that bind or benefit successive owners of a property, such as a restrictive building covenant in a recorded deed that would affect all future owners of the property.

rural A land-use classification pertaining to rustic areas, as opposed to urban areas; land devoted to the pursuit of agriculture.

S

safe harbor rule
1. An area of protection, for example, the rules under IRS 3508 that protect a real estate broker from attack by the IRS for failing to withhold taxes when treating his or her salespeople as independent contractors.
2. IRS standards for a delayed 1031 exchange in which an intermediary can hold title pending the identification and acquisition of the replacement property within set time limits.

sale-leaseback A real estate financing technique whereby a property owner sells the property to an investor or lender and, at the same time, leases it

S

back; the lease used is usually a full net lease that extends over a period of time long enough for the investor-lender to recover his or her funds and to make a fair profit on the investment, and the arrangement allows the original property owner to "pull out" his or her equity from the property and the rents paid to the investor are fully deductible expenses in the year in which they are incurred.

sale of leased property A transaction in which an owner of property who has given a lease to one person may sell the leased property to another, although the buyer takes the property subject to the existing lease.

sales-assessment ratio The ratio of the assessed value of real property to its selling price.

sales associate Licensed salesperson or broker who works for a broker.

sales kit An assortment of information about property to be sold.

salesperson(s) Any licensed person who, for a compensation or valuable consideration, is employed either directly or indirectly by a licensed real estate broker to perform certain acts: to sell, offer to sell, buy, offer to buy; negotiate the purchase, sale or exchange of real estate; lease, rent, or offer to rent any real estate, or to negotiate leases thereof or improvements thereon.

S

salvage value
1. The estimated amount for which an asset can be sold at the end of its useful life for pre-1981 property, now disregarded under the Economic Recovery Tax Act of 1981.
2. The value of a structure to be relocated to another site.

sandwich lease A leasehold estate in which the sandwich party leases the property from the fee owner or another lessee and then sublets to the tenant in possession, thereby maintaining a middle, or "sandwich," position.

sanitary sewer system A sewer system that carries only domestic water, usually an underground pipe or tunnel to carry off wastes and effluents.

satellite tenant A smaller shopping center tenant that is relatively dependent on the ability of a larger anchor or prime tenant to attract business into the center.

satisfaction The payment of a debt or obligation such as a judgment.

satisfaction of mortgage A certificate issued by the mortgagee when a mortgage is paid in full; the document is called a *discharge* or *release of mortgage,* or a *satisfaction piece.*

savings and loan association (S&L) A financial institution whose principal function is to promote thrift and home ownership, commonly called a *Savings Association*; active participants in the home loan mortgage market.

Savings Association Insurance Fund (SAIF) The fund that insures deposits of savings and loan associations operated through the Federal Deposit Insurance Corporation (FDIC).

scarcity A lack of supply of some type of real property, the supply of which cannot readily be increased; value increases when demand exceeds supply.

scenic easement An easement created to preserve a property in its natural state.

schematics Preliminary architectural drawings and sketches often prepared at the planning stages of a project; basic layouts not containing the final details of design.

scope of authority A rule of agency law holding that a principal is liable to third parties for all wrongful acts of his or her agent committed while transacting the principal's business.

S corporation A small domestic corporation that has elected to be treated more like a partnership for tax purposes, designated by IRS Form 2553; allowing a business to operate in corporate form and yet not pay a corporate tax, thus avoiding the double tax feature of corporate ownership; stockholders are taxed on their share of the corporation's income, whether or not it is distributed.

seal An embossed impression on paper caused by a metal die used to authenticate a document or attest to a signature, as with a corporate or notary seal.

S

sealed and delivered A phrase indicating that a transferor has received adequate consideration as evidenced by his or her voluntary delivery.

seasoned loan A loan borrowed by someone who has a stable and consistent history of payments under the terms of the loan.

secondary financing A junior mortgage placed on property to help finance the purchase price, such as a purchase-money second mortgage taken back by the seller to assist a purchaser who has difficulty in making a large down payment.

secondary mortgage market A market for the purchase and sale of existing mortgages designed to provide greater liquidity for selling mortgages; also called **secondary money market**, not to be confused with secondary financing.

second-generation leasing A term used in the shopping center industry to describe a leasing of space in buildings already constructed and previously occupied by other tenants.

second mortgage A mortgage (or trust deed) that is junior or subordinate to a first mortgage; typically, an additional loan imposed on top of the first mortgage, taken out when the borrower needs more money.

secret profit Refers to a broker making an undisclosed profit at the seller's expense.

Section 8 Program A federal rent subsidy program for low-income and moderate-income tenants to choose privately owned rental housing and is divided into two programs: tenant-based and project-based.

Section 203(b) The centerpiece of home mortgage insurance offered by the Federal Housing Administration; 203(b) is also available to those who live in underserved areas where mortgages may be harder to obtain.

secured party The person having the security interest, such as the mortgagee, the vendee, or the pledgee.

Securities and Exchange Commission (SEC) An independent regulatory agency that aims to protect investors and to ensure that the securities markets function fairly and honestly by enforcing securities laws through sanctions. The agency's decisions can be reviewed by the United States Court of Appeals.

security Evidence of obligations to pay money or of rights to participate in earnings and distribution of corporate, trust, or other property; securities are regulated by both state and federal law.

security agreement A security document that creates a lien on personal property (chattels), including chattels intended to be affixed to land as fixtures; known as a *chattel mortgage* before the adoption of the Uniform Commercial Code (UCC).

security deposit Money deposited by or for the tenant with the landlord, to be held by the landlord for the following purposes: (1) to remedy

S

tenant defaults for damage to the premises (accidental or intentional), for failure to pay rent due or for failure to return keys at the end of the tenancy; (2) to clean the dwelling so as to place it in as fit a condition as when the tenant commenced possession, considering normal wear and tear; and (3) to compensate for damages caused by a tenant who wrongfully quits the dwelling unit.

seisin Actual possession of property by one who claims rightful ownership of a freehold interest therein; generally considered to be synonymous with ownership.

seizure The taking of property by the government when the property is being used to conduct illegal activities such as drug dealing.

seller financing Financing provided by the owner/seller of real estate, who takes back a secured note.

seller's market An economic situation that favors the seller because the demand for property exceeds the supply.

selling broker The broker who procures the buyer.

semiannual Occurring twice each year, as in semiannual tax payments.

semi-detached dwelling A residence that shares one wall with an adjoining building.

S

separate property Property held individually, as opposed to community property or property held jointly.

service of process The legal act of notifying the defendant of an impending lawsuit and the delivery to him or her of the summons and complaint in the action.

servicing As specified in a servicing agreement, a mortgage banker's duties performed for a fee as loan correspondent.

servient estate Land on which an easement or other right exists in favor of an adjacent property (called a *dominant estate*); also referred to as a *servient tenement*.

servitude A burden or charge on an estate.

setback Zoning restrictions on the amount of land required surrounding improvements; the amount of space required between the lot line and the building line.

settlement
1. The act of adjusting and prorating the various credits, charges, and settlement costs to conclude a real estate transaction, also called closing.
2. The act of compromising in a dispute or a lawsuit; such an act is usually not an admission of liability.

severalty Sole ownership of real property.

severance The act of removing something attached to land or of terminating a relationship.

S

severance damages A recognition for the loss of value in the remaining property caused by the partial taking of real property under the state, federal, or local government's power of eminent domain.

shall In common statutory language, meaning that which is required by law.

shared appreciation A form of participation mortgage in which the lender shares in the appreciation of a property mortgaged if and when the property is sold.

shell lease A lease in which a tenant leases the unfinished shell of a building, as in a new shopping center, and agrees to complete construction by installing ceilings, plumbing, heating and air-conditioning systems, and electrical wiring.

sheriff's deed Deed given by a court to effect the sale of property to satisfy a judgment. (See **deed**)

shopping The practice of negotiating a deal and then attempting to find another deal with better terms.

shopping center A modern classification of retail stores, characterized by off-street parking and clusters of stores, subject to a uniform development plan and usually with careful analysis given to the proper merchant mix; usually classified by size, mix, number of families served, and so forth.

shoreline The dividing line between private land and public beach on beachfront property.

S

short-form document A brief document that refers to a contract such as a mortgage (called a *fictitious mortgage*), lease, option, or sales contract. Simply recites the fact that a contract has been made between the parties covering certain described premises, thus satisfying the requirements of recordation yet keeping secret the essential terms and conditions of the transaction.

short rate A higher periodic rate charged for a shorter term than that originally contracted.

short sale A sale of secured real property that produces less money than is owed the lender; also called a short pay, in that the lender releases its mortgage or trust deed so that the property can be sold free and clear to the new purchaser.

short-term capital gain A tax term for gain from the sale or exchange of a capital asset held for one year or less.

should Common statutory language meaning that which is recommended but not required by law.

sick building syndrome (SBS) A label given to indoor air quality problems in commercial and industrial buildings that lead to symptoms that affect building occupants in the building and which go away when they leave the building and cannot be traced to specific pollutants or sources within the building.

signage Slang term for signs, typically referring to whether there are any restrictions of the size or placement of signs on the property.

S

signature Use of any name, including a trade or fictitious name, upon an instrument, or any word or mark used as and intended to be a written signature.

signs Printed display boards frequently used to indicate the availability of real estate on the market; signs must comply with all advertising regulations and generally, an owner's consent is required before placing a For Sale sign on the property.

silent second An unrecorded second mortgage, typically held secret from the underlying first mortgagee.

silent partner An inactive partner in business.

simple interest Interest computed on the principal balance only and not additionally on unpaid but previously earned interest.

single agency The practice of representing either the buyer or the seller but never both in the same transaction.

single-family residence A structure maintained and used as a single dwelling unit, designed for occupancy by one family, as in a private home; opposite of a condominium, apartment building, or PUD.

single licensing A state law requirement that all real estate agents have the same license rather than the traditional method of licensing salespersons and brokers.

sinking fund   A fund created to amass enough money gradually to satisfy a debt or to meet a specific requirement; a fund designed to accumulate money to a predetermined amount at the end of a stated period of time, such as a fund set up to repay debentures.

site   The position, situation, or location of a piece of land.

site office   A temporary place of realty business other than the principal place of business or branch office, from which real estate activities are conducted that relate to a specific piece of real property (open house), real estate condominium project, or real estate subdivision.

situs
  1. The preference by people for a certain location.
  2. The place where something exists or originates; the place where something (as a right) is held to be located in law.

slander of title   A tort or civil wrong in which a person maliciously makes disparaging, untrue statements concerning another's title to property, thus causing injury.

slum clearance   The clearing of old, decrepit buildings so the land may be put to a better, more productive use.

Small Business Administration (SBA)   A federal agency created to administer the federal government's program for the preservation and development of small business concerns.

small claims court A division of the district court whose jurisdiction is limited to cases of claims not exceeding a certain amount, for example, $1,000 exclusive of interest and costs which provides an inexpensive and speedy forum for the disposition of minor controversies.

soft money

1. The money financed under a purchase-money mortgage as a part of the purchase price.
2. Tax-deductible items such as carrying charges (interest, real estate taxes, and ground rents) incurred while holding unimproved property or during construction.

soil bank A program administered by the Commodity Stabilization Service of the U.S. Department of Agriculture in which farmers are paid to divert land from production of unneeded crops to conservation uses.

solar easement An easement designed to protect an owner's access to light and the rays of the sun.

Soldiers and Sailors Civil Relief Act (SSCRA) A federal law designed to protect persons in the mil'itary service from loss of property when their ability to meet their obligations has been materially affected by the requirements of their military service.

sole proprietorship A method of owning a business in which one person owns the entire business and reports all profits and losses directly on his or her personal income tax return, as contrasted with corporate, joint, or partnership ownership.

spec home
1. A home built on speculation.
2. A model home.

special agent One authorized by a principal to perform a particular act or transaction, without contemplation of continuity of service as with a general agent; ordinarily a real estate broker is a special agent appointed by the seller to find a ready, willing, and able buyer for a particular property as is an attorney-in-fact under a limited power of attorney.

special assessment A tax or levy customarily imposed against only those specific parcels of realty that benefit from a proposed public improvement, as opposed to a general tax on the entire community.

special benefit The value added to a specific property or a limited number of properties as a result of some government improvement.

special conditions Specific provisions in a real estate sales contract that must be satisfied before the contract is binding.

special lien A lien or charge against a specific parcel of property, such as a mortgage, attachment, or mechanic's lien.

S

special-purpose property   A combination of land and improvements with only one highest and best use because of some special design, such as a church, nursing home, school, post office, or hospital.

special-use permit   Permission from the local zoning authority granting a land use identified as a special exception in the zoning ordinance.

special warranty deed   A deed in which the grantor warrants or guarantees the title only against defects arising during the period of his or her tenure and ownership of the property and not against defects existing before that time.

specifications   Written instructions to a building contractor containing all the necessary information of a proposed construction.

specific performance   An action brought in a court of equity in special cases to compel a party to carry out the terms of a contract.

speculator
1. One who analyzes a real property market and acquires properties with the expectation that prices will greatly increase, at which time he or she can sell at a large profit.
2. An owner/builder who constructs homes ("spec homes") in the expectation that he or she will find willing buyers when the homes are *completed* (rather than have a specific buyer ready at the time construction begins).

S

spin-off The transfer of a company's assets to a recently formed subsidiary.

spite fence A fence erected and of such height or type as to annoy a neighbor.

split financing A financing situation in which the land and the improvements are financed separately, often used by developers to obtain greater total permanent financing than would ordinarily be available by typical conventional financing.

split-rate Capitalization rates applied separately to land and improvements, to determine the value of each.

splitting fees The act of sharing compensation.

spot survey A survey that illustrates the locations, sizes, and shapes of buildings, improvements, and easements located on a property, as well as those on any neighboring property that may encroach on the surveyed property.

spot zoning A change in the local zoning ordinance permitting a particular use inconsistent with the zoning classification of the area; the reclassification of a small area of land in such a manner as to disturb the tenor of the surrounding neighborhood, such as a change to permit one multiunit structure in an area zoned for single-family residential use; also called a variance.

square-foot method A method of estimating a building's construction, reproduction, or replacement costs whereby the structure's square-foot

S

floor area is multiplied by an appropriate construction cost per square foot.

squatter's right The right of a person in adverse possession of real property; must generally be actual, open, notorious, exclusive, and continuous for a period of time prescribed by statute.

staging

1. A temporary scaffolding used to support workers and materials during construction.
2. A process by which the real estate licensee assists the seller in selecting, designing, rearranging, or modifying the home in order to better show it to buyers, hopefully, to produce a better sale price; also called prepping a property.

staging area An area where material, apparatus, equipment, or merchandise is collected or assembled before it is moved to where it will finally be used or stored.

staking A method of identifying the boundaries of a parcel of land by placing stakes or pins in the ground or by painting marks on stone walls or rocks.

standard metropolitan statistical area (SMSA) An important designation given by the federal Office of Management and Budget to counties with at least one central city of 50,000 or more residents.

standby fee A substantial sum paid by a borrower at the time of issuance of a standby commitment letter, as a charge for the lender's risk and

S

responsibility in committing to the loan which is forfeited if the loan is not closed within a specified time.

standby loan An arrangement whereby the lender agrees to keep a certain amount of money available to the borrower, usually a developer, for a specified period of time; similar to an option on a loan, because the developer has the right to borrow the money but is not obligated to do so.

standing loan

1. A commitment by the interim or construction lender to keep the money he or she has already funded in the project for a specified period of time after the expiration of the interim loan, usually until permanent takeout financing is secured.
2. A straight mortgage, i.e., one that calls for payments of interest only with no amortization during its term and the entire principal becoming due at maturity.

starter

1. Reference to an earlier title report on a particular piece of real property.
2. A person's first residence or other real estate investment.

starts A term commonly used to indicate the number of residential units begun within a stated period of time.

S

state-certified appraiser An appraiser certified or licensed according to certification requirements set by the state.

statement of record A document that must be filed with a HUD registration of subdivided land intended to be sold using any means of interstate commerce.

statute A law enacted by Congress (federal law) or by a state legislature (state law), as opposed to judicial or common law; statutory law as opposed to case law.

statute of frauds State law that requires certain contracts to be in writing and signed by the party to be charged (or held) to the agreement in order to be legally enforceable.

statute of limitations That law pertaining to the period of time within which certain actions must be brought to court.

statutory law Law created by the enactment of legislation, as opposed to case law created by judicial decision.

steering The illegal practice of channeling home seekers interested in equivalent properties to particular areas, either to maintain the homogeneity of an area or to change the character of an area to create a speculative situation.

stepped-up basis The new basis of property acquired from a decedent, equal to the value as finally determined by the IRS of the property transferred on the date of death, or on an alternate valuation date for federal estate tax purposes (six months after the date of death), or the fair market value where no estate tax return is filed.

step-up lease A lease with fixed rent for an initial term and a predetermined rent increase at specified intervals and/or increases based on periodic appraisals.

stick-built on-site Construction by an on-site builder who builds with raw materials that are delivered to the construction site which are then measured, cut, and assembled by skilled craftspeople.

stigmatized property A property regarded as undesirable because of events that occurred there; also called psychologically impacted property.

straight-line method A method of depreciation, also called the age-life method, computed by dividing the adjusted basis of a property by the number of years of estimated remaining useful life.

straight note A promissory note evidencing a loan in which payments of interest only are made periodically during the term of the note, with the principal payment due in one lump sum upon maturity.

straw man One who purchases property for another so as to conceal the identity of the real purchaser; a dummy purchaser; a nominee; a front.

S

structural defects In residential homes, actual damage to the load-bearing portion of a home that affects its load-bearing function and vitally affects the use of the home for residential purposes.

structural density The ratio of the total ground floor area of a building to the total land area.

structure Something built or constructed; an improvement.

studio See **efficiency unit or apartment.**

subagent An agent of a person who is already acting as an agent for a principal.

subagreement of sale An agreement of sale (contract for deed) between the original vendee of an agreement of sale and a new purchaser; under such an agreement there is no contractual relationship between the new purchaser (subvendee) and the owner of the property (original vendor).

subcontractor A builder or contractor who enters into an agreement with the prime contractor to perform a special portion of the construction work but who does not deal directly with the owner although if not paid by the prime contractor, can assert a mechanic's lien against the property.

subdivider An owner whose land is divided into two or more lots and offered for disposition.

subdivision Land that is divided or is proposed to be divided for the purpose of disposition into two or more lots, parcels, units, or interests.

S

subdivision registration law Laws requiring subdivision registration to protect prospective purchasers from the deceptive practices and abuses once common in the unregulated sale of greater numbers of unimproved lots.

subjective value The amount a specific person might pay to possess a property; also called **personal value** as opposed to **objective value,** or what a reasonable person might be expected to pay for the same property.

subject property A reference to the real property under discussion, or the real property under appraisal.

"subject to" clause The clause in a contract for sale setting forth any contingencies or special conditions of purchase and sale, such as contingent upon obtaining financing, approving leases, securing certain zoning, and similar requirements.

"subject to" mortgage A grantee taking title to a real property "subject to" a mortgage is not personally liable to the mortgagee for payment of the mortgage note; however if the grantor/mortgagor defaults in paying the note, the grantee could lose the property, and thus his or her equity, in a foreclosure sale.

sublease A lease given by a lessee for a portion of the leasehold interest, while the lessee retains some reversionary interest.

submittal notice Written notice by a broker to a seller with whom he or she has a listing agreement,

S

stating that the broker has shown the seller's property and indicating the prospect's name, address, and the selling price quoted; this notice is especially important in open listing situations to avoid problems with regard to procuring cause.

subordination agreement An agreement whereby a holder of a prior superior mortgage agrees to subordinate or give up his or her priority position to an existing or anticipated future lien.

subordination clause A clause in which the holder of a mortgage permits a subsequent mortgage to take priority; the act of yielding priority.

subpoena A legal process ordering a witness to appear and give testimony under penalty of law.

subpoena duces tecum A court order to produce books, records, and other documents.

subprime loan A loan made to persons with lower credit ratings than acceptable in regular loans, based on the fact that lenders can negotiate the interest rate and discount in their efforts to make substantial profits.

subrogation The substitution of a third person in place of a creditor to whose rights the third person succeeds in relation to the debt.

subscribe To place one's signature at the end of a document.

subscription An agreement to buy a new securities issue.

subsequent bona fide purchaser One who purchases an interest in real property without notice, actual or constructive, of any other superior rights in the property.

subsidized housing Residential developments for low-income families that are insured or financed in part by a governmental agency.

subsidy Monetary grants by the government or a seller or developer made to reduce the cost of one or more of the housing components—land, labor, management, materials—to lower the cost of housing to the occupant.

subsidy rent The difference between the developer's cash out-of-pocket annual costs allocable to a particular tenant's space and the tenant's minimum rental.

substantial improvement For tax purposes, any improvement made to a building at least three years after the building was placed in service; over a two-year period, the amounts added to the capital account of the building (not repairs) must be at least 25 percent of the adjusted basis of the building as of the first day of that period.

substitution A principle of value that states that the maximum value of a property tends to be set by the cost of acquiring, through purchase or construction, an equally desirable and valuable substitute property, assuming no costly delay is encountered in making the substitution.

S

substitution of collateral Provision in a mortgage to permit the mortgagor to obtain a release of the original collateral by replacement with other collateral acceptable to the mortgagee.

subsurface easement An easement permitting the use of belowground space for such purposes as power lines, sewers, tunnels; also called a **subsurface right.**

successors and assigns Words of limitation used in deeds to corporations, referring to those who succeed to or to whom the corporation's rights in the property are transferred.

summary possession A legal process, also called **actual eviction,** used by a landlord to regain possession of the leased premises if the tenant has breached the lease or is holding over after the termination of tenancy.

summation approach The value derived by adding the estimated value of improvements to the estimated value of the site as of the date of the appraisal.

summons A legal notice that a lawsuit has commenced against a defendant.

superadequacy Functional obsolescence caused by an improvement or structural component whose cost exceeds its value.

Superfund The nickname given to the fund that focuses on the cleanup of releases of hazardous substances on property; it creates significant legal exposure based on strict liability for owners, land-lords, and, sometimes, lenders.

supply and demand An economic valuation principle that states market value is determined by the interaction of the forces of supply and demand in the appropriate market as of the date of the appraisal; supply is low, price is high, although when supply is high and there is little demand, price is low.

surcharge
1. Additional rent charged to tenants who consume utility services in excess of the amounts allowed in the terms of the lease.
2. An additional charge imposed by the Federal Reserve Bank on member banks that borrow money too frequently.

surety One who becomes a guarantor for another.

surface water Diffused storm water, as contrasted to a concentrated flow within a stream.

surrender A premature conveyance of a possessory estate to a person having a future interest, as when a lessee surrenders his or her leasehold interest to the owner of the reversion interest, the lessor, before the normal expiration of the lease; as opposed to an abandonment of the lease.

survey The process by which boundaries are measured and land areas determined; the on-site measurement of lot lines, dimensions, and position of houses in a lot, including the determination of any existing encroachments, easements, party walls, and compliance with setback requirements.

survivorship, right of The special feature of a joint tenancy whereby all title, right, and interest of a decedent joint tenant in certain property passes to the surviving joint tenants by operation of law, free from claims of heirs and creditors of the decedent.

suspension A period of enforced inactivity; for example, if the real estate license is suspended for a violation of the licensing law, the licensee is prohibited from engaging in real estate activities for the purpose of earning a commission or fee.

sweat equity A popular expression for equity created in a property by the performance of work or labor by the purchaser or borrower that directly increases the value of the property.

sweetheart contract A slang expression to describe a situation where a developer hires a thinly disguised subsidiary company to manage the developer's project.

swing loan A short-term loan used to enable the purchaser of a new property to purchase that property on the strength of the equity from the property the purchaser is now selling.

syndication A descriptive term for a group of two or more people united for the purpose of making and operating an investment; syndication is not a form of legal ownership, simply a term used to describe multiple ownership of an investment.

systems-built A term used by premium-home builders to describe factory-built construction to avoid the stigma attached to manufactured or prefab homes.

tacking
1. Adding or combining successive periods of continuous occupation of real property by adverse possessors, thus enabling one not in possession for the entire required statutory period to establish a claim of adverse possession.
2. A carryover of holding periods for tax purposes.

take down To borrow or draw against funds committed by a lender earlier, as in a construction loan.

take off The estimation of materials needed to construct a building.

takeout financing Long-term permanent financing.

taking Reference to the "takings clause" of the Fifth Amendment, which states ". . . nor shall private property be taken for public use, without just compensation."

T

tax and lien search A title search issued to cover property registered in the Torrens system.

tax abatement A reduction, for a stated period of time, of the taxes of a property owner; a downside is higher taxes when the abatement is lifted.

tax base
1. For property tax purposes, the assessed valuation of all real property within an area subject to taxes excluding exempt church-owned or government-owned property.
2. For income tax purposes, the net taxable income.

tax bracket The rate at which a taxpayer pays tax on income above a set amount.

tax certificate The document issued to a person as a receipt for paying the delinquent taxes on real property owned by another, entitling the person to receive a deed to the property if the property is not redeemed within a specified period.

tax clearance A form required by the state to be filed by a decedent's estate when real property is owned in that state, verifying that there are no outstanding inheritance tax liens on the property.

tax credit A dollar-for-dollar offset against taxes due often used as incentives to develop low-income housing, historic properties, or housing for the elderly, or to encourage businesses to make alterations in compliance with the ADA accessibility rules.

tax deed The instrument used to convey legal title to property sold by a governmental unit for nonpayment of taxes.

tax-deferred exchange A transaction in which some or all of the realized gain from the exchange of one property for another may not have to be immediately recognized for tax purposes; the exchange is not a tax-free transaction; the payment of taxes is simply deferred to a later transfer.

tax lien A statutory lien imposed against real property for nonpayment of taxes, which remains on the property until the taxes are paid, even if the real estate is conveyed to another person.

tax map A map drawn to scale showing the location of real property, tax keys, size, shape, and dimensions and so on, for convenience of identification, valuation, and assessment.

tax participation clause A clause in a commercial lease that requires the tenant to pay a pro rata share of any increases in taxes or assessments above an established base year.

tax rate The rate that is applied to the assessed value of a property to arrive at the amount of annual property tax.

Tax Relief Act of 1997 Tax rules that provided for tax relief for persons selling their personal property or investment property.

tax roll Public records showing all taxable property, tax amounts, assessed valuations, and millage rates.

tax sale The sale of real property by a governmental unit to satisfy unpaid real property tax liens, frequently followed by a statutory period of redemption.

tax search A specific part of a title search that determines whether there are any unpaid taxes or special assessments that may be a lien against the property under search.

tax shelter A phrase often used to describe some of the tax advantages of real estate or other investments; tax reform in 1986 significantly limited the use of tax shelter losses to reduce taxable income from other sources such as salary, interest, and dividends.

tax stop clause A lease article providing that the lessee will pay any increase in taxes over a base or initial year's taxes; also referred to as a *tax-escalation clause*.

teaser rate mortgage An adjustable-rate mortgage with an interest rate initially set below the market rate.

Telephone Consumer Protection Act A law designed to restrict unsolicited calls by telemarketers.

tenancy at sufferance A tenancy (or estate) that exists when a tenant wrongfully holds over after the expiration of a lease without the landlord's consent, as where the tenant fails to surrender possession after termination of the lease.

tenancy at will A tenancy (or estate) in which a person holds or occupies real estate with the permission of the owner, for a term of unspecified or uncertain duration: i.e., there is no fixed term to the tenancy.

tenancy by the entirety (entireties) A special joint tenancy between a lawfully married husband and wife, which places all title to property (real or personal) into the marital unit; upon the death of one spouse, the survivor succeeds to the entire property to the exclusion of heirs and creditors of the deceased spouse and without the need for probate.

tenancy for life A freehold estate of uncertain duration, which is not an estate of inheritance; a life estate.

tenancy for years A less-than-freehold estate (or tenancy) in which the property is leased for a definite, fixed period of time, whether 60 days, any fraction of a year, a year, or ten years.

tenancy in common A form of concurrent ownership of property between two or more persons, in which each has an undivided interest in the whole property; unlike a joint tenancy, there is no right of survivorship in a tenancy in common, so when one of the cotenants dies, the interest passes to his or her heirs or beneficiaries and not the surviving tenants in common; thus the interest is subject to probate.

tenancy in partnership A partnership is an association of two or more persons for the purpose of carrying on a business as co-owners and sharing in the profits and losses.

T

tenancy in severalty Ownership of property vested in one person alone (or one corporation), rather than held jointly with another; also called **several tenancy** or **sole tenancy;** when the sole owner dies, the property is probated and passes to his or her heirs or devisees.

tenant In general, one who exclusively holds or possesses property, such as a life tenant or a tenant for years; commonly used to refer to a lessee under a lease; however, *tenant* refers to an occupant, not necessarily a renter.

tenant alternative costs The costs of construction and remodeling needed to make the premises usable by a particular tenant paid by the owner or the tenant or may be shared by both as a result of negotiations.

tenant contributions All costs for which the tenant is responsible over and above the contract rent specified in the lease.

tenant mix The selection and location of retail tenants so as to maximize the income to the lessor and stimulate business in general.

tenant union A local organization of residential tenants working for their common interests and rights.

tender An unconditional offer by one of the parties to a contract to perform his or her part of the bargain.

tenement

1. A common-law real estate term describing those real property rights of a permanent nature that relate to the land and pass with a conveyance of the land, such as buildings and improvements; those things affixed to the land. Tenements include not only land but also corporeal and incorporeal rights in real property.

2. In modern usage, the term refers to apartment buildings, especially the more run-down, old buildings in urban areas.

tenure A common-law term indicating the manner in which land is held, such as a fee simple or leasehold.

term

1. A length of time, found in a mortgage, a lease, or an option.

2. A provision or condition in a contract.

termination of listing The cancellation of a broker-principal employment contract by death of either party, expiration, mutual agreement, sufficient written notice, completion of the task, condemnation or destruction of the subject property, bankruptcy of either party, abandonment, revocation by the principal, or a change in law that prohibits the current use of the property.

termination statement A document recorded to cancel a financing statement filed under the provisions of the Uniform Commercial Code.

T

termite inspection A visible check of the premises for the presence of termites, usually performed by a licensed exterminator.

term mortgage A short-term mortgage securing a loan that requires interest-only payments until the maturity date, at which time the entire principal is due and payable.

testator A person who makes a last will and testament; one who dies leaving a will and is said to have died *testate*.

thin market A real estate market in which there are few buyers and sellers and a slow turnover of properties.

third party A person such as the broker or escrow agent who is not party to a contract but who may be affected by it; one who is not a principal to the transaction.

tidewater land Land beneath the ocean from low-tide mark to a state's outer territorial limits.

tie-in contract A contract in which one transaction depends on another.

tight money market An economic situation in which the supply of money is limited and the demand for money is high, as evidenced by high interest rates.

"time is of the essence" A contract clause that emphasizes punctual performance as an essential requirement of the contract; thus any party that does not perform within the specified time period is in default.

time-price differential The difference between a property's purchase price and the higher total price the same property would cost if purchased on an installment basis (including finance charges); disclosure of which is required under the Truth-in-Lending Act.

time-sharing A modern approach to communal ownership and use of real estate that permits multiple purchasers to buy undivided interests in real property (usually in a resort condominium or hotel) with a right to use the facility for a fixed or variable time period.

time value of money An economic principle that the worth of a dollar received today is greater than the worth of a dollar received in the future.

title The right to or ownership of land; the evidence of the right to an estate.

title insurance A comprehensive indemnity contract under which a title insurance company warrants to make good a loss arising through defects in title to real estate or any liens or encumbrances; title insurance protects a policyholder against loss from some occurrence that has already happened, not a future event. An *owner's policy* is issued for the benefit of the owner, and a *lender's policy* is issued for the benefit of a mortgage lender and any future holder of the loan.

title report A preliminary report of the current record title to a property showing only the current state of the title along with the recorded objections to clear title such as unpaid mortgages and easements on which title insurance policy is issued.

title search An examination of the public records to determine what, if any, defects there are in the chain of title; usually performed by an experienced title company or abstracter.

title-theory states States in which the law considers the mortgagee to have legal title to the mortgaged property, and the mortgagor to have equitable title; under title theory, a mortgagee has the right to possession and rents of the mortgaged property upon default.

tolling The suspension or interruption of the running of the statute of limitations period.

topography The nature of the surface of the land; the contour.

Torrens system A legal system for the registration of land, used to verify the ownership and encumbrances (except tax liens), without the necessity of an additional search of the public records adopted by approximately ten states.

tort A negligent or intentional wrongful act arising from breach of duty created by law and not contract; violation of a legal right; a civil wrong such as negligence, libel, nuisance, trespass, slander of title, or false imprisonment.

town house A type of dwelling unit normally having two floors, with the living area and kitchen on the base floor and the bedrooms located on the second floor; a series of individual houses having architectural unity and a common wall between each unit, popular in cluster housing, and often employ the use of party walls and shared common grounds.

township A division of territory, used in the government (rectangular) survey system of land description, that is six miles square; contains 36 sections, each of which is one mile square.

track record
1. The previous operating results of a sponsor (or developer) or a real estate project.
2. The history of a real estate syndicator.

tract A lot or parcel of land; a certain development.

tract house A house mass-produced according to the plans of the builder, as one of many residences in a subdivision that are very similar in style, materials, and price.

tract index An index of records of title according to the description of the property conveyed, mortgaged, or otherwise encumbered or disposed of.

trade fixture An article of personal property annexed or affixed to leased premises by the tenant as a necessary part of the tenant's trade or business; trade fixtures are removable by the tenant before expiration of the lease, and the tenant is responsible for any damages caused by their removal.

trade-in An agreement by a developer or broker to accept from a buyer a designated piece of real property as a part of the purchase price of another property.

trading up Buying or exchanging for something more expensive than what is currently owned.

transaction broker A nonagency relationship allowed in states that have designed a category of service where the agent represents neither the buyer nor seller in the transaction, treating both as customers.

transfer certificate of title (TCT) A duplicate Torrens system certificate of title.

transfer of development rights (TDR) A concept of land-use planning that looks at land development rights as being a part of the bundle of individual rights of land ownership; any one of these rights may be separated from the rest and transferred to someone else, leaving the original owner with all other remaining rights of ownership.

transfer tax (conveyance fee) A state tax imposed on the transfer or conveyance of realty or any realty interest by means of deed, lease, sublease, assignment, contract for deed, or similar instrument.

treble damages Damages provided for by statute in certain cases, as in an antitrust suit; actual damages may be tripled.

trespass Any wrongful, unauthorized invasion of land ownership by a person having no lawful right or title to enter on the property.

T

triple A tenant A commercial tenant with a top credit rating, especially desirable as an anchor tenant in a shopping center.

triple-net lease A net-net-net lease where, in addition to the stipulated rent, the lessee assumes payment of all expenses associated with the operation of the property, such as taxes and insurance, and all operating expenses, including costs of maintenance and repair. In some cases, the triple-net tenant even pays the interest payments on the lessor's mortgage on the property leased.

triplex A building comprised of three dwelling units.

trust An arrangement whereby legal title to property is transferred by the *grantor* (or *trustor*) to a person called a *trustee,* to be held and managed by that person for the benefit of another, called a *beneficiary.*

trust beneficiary The person for whom a trust is created.

trustee
1. One who holds property in trust for another as a fiduciary and is charged with the duty to protect, preserve, and enhance the value and the highest and best use of the trust property.
2. One who holds property in trust for another to secure the performance of an obligation.

T

trustee in bankruptcy One appointed by the court to preserve and manage the assets of a party in bankruptcy.

trust fund account An account set up by a broker, attorney, or other agent at a bank or other recognized depository, into which the broker deposits all funds entrusted to the agent by the principal or others; also called an **earnest money** or **escrow account.**

Truth-in-Lending Act (TIL) A body of federal law to ensure that borrowers and customers in need of consumer credit are given meaningful information with respect to the cost of credit so they can more readily compare the various credit terms available to them; TIL does not establish any set maximum or minimum interest rates or require any charges for credit.

tsunami damage Damage caused by tidal-wave action, which is only covered by flood insurance, not a typical homeowners' policy.

turnkey project A development term meaning the complete construction package from ground breaking to building completion.

turnover
1. The frequency with which real property in a given area is sold and resold.
2. The rate at which tenants move into and out of a rental building.

unbalanced improvement An improvement that is not the highest and best use for the site, either an overimprovement or an underimprovement.

unconscionability A legal doctrine whereby a court refuses to enforce a contract that was grossly unfair or unscrupulous at the time it was made; a contract offensive to the public conscience.

underground storage tanks (USTs) A tank and any underground piping connected to the tank having 10 percent or more of its volume beneath the surface of the ground.

underimprovement An improvement that, because of its deficiency in size or cost, is not the highest and best use of the site.

underlying financing A mortgage or deed of trust that takes precedence over subsequent liens, such as contracts for deed or mortgages on the same property.

undersigned The person whose name is signed at the end of a document; the subscriber.

undertenant One who holds property under one who is already a tenant, as in a sublease; a subtenant.

underwater loan A term indicating a higher loan balance than what can be realized by the sale of the property.

underwriter

1. In insurance, a person who selects risks to be solicited and then rates the acceptability of the risks solicited.
2. As applied to real property securities, a person who has purchased securities from the issuer with the intention to offer, or who actually sells or distributes, the securities for the issuer.
3. A person working for a lender who reviews a loan application and makes a recommendation to the loan committee.

underwriting The analysis of the extent of risk assumed in connection with a loan.

undisclosed agency A situation where an agent deals with a third person without notifying that person of the agency.

undistributed taxable income Income received by an S corporation that, although it is not distributed to the shareholders, is taxed as part of the shareholder's income.

undivided interest That interest a co-owner has in property that carries with it a right to possession of the whole property along with the other co-owners; although the undivided interests may be equal, as in a joint tenancy, or unequal, as sometimes in a tenancy in common, no owner has the right to any specific part of the whole.

undue influence Strong enough persuasion to completely overpower the free will of another and prevent him or her from acting intelligently and voluntarily.

unearned income Income derived from sources other than personal services, such as rents, dividends, and royalties.

unearned increment An increase in value to real property that comes about from forces outside the influence and control of the property owner.

unencumbered property A property that is free and clear of liens and other encumbrances; a "free and clear" property.

unenforceable contract A contract that was valid when made but either cannot be proved or will not be enforced by a court.

unethical Lacking in moral principles; failing to conform to an accepted code of behavior.

unfair and deceptive practices Sales practices that do not involve deception but are still illegal under the regulations of the Federal Trade Commission (FTC).

unfinished office space Space in a "shell" condition excluding dividing walls, ceiling, lighting, air-conditioning, floor covering, and the like.

uniform and model acts Laws approved by the National Conference of Commissioners on Uniform State Laws and proposed for adoption in the individual states.

U

Uniform Building Code A code published by the International Conference of Building Officials now being replaced by the codes developed by the International Code Council.

Uniform Commercial Code (UCC) A body of law that attempts to codify and make uniform throughout the country all law relating to commercial transactions, such as conditional sales contracts, pledges, and chattel mortgages; including personal property transactions, negotiable securities, and commercial paper.

Uniform Commercial-Industrial Appraisal Report (UCIAR) A standard appraisal report form for appraising commercial and industrial property.

uniformity An appraisal term used in tax assessment practice to describe assessed values that have the same relationship to market value and thus imply the equalization of the tax burden.

Uniform Limited Partnership Act A model act, adopted in whole or in part by many states, establishing the legality of the limited partnership form of ownership and providing that realty may be held in the name of the limited partnership.

Uniform Partnership Act (UPA) A model act, adopted in whole or in part by most states, establishing the legality of the partnership form of ownership and providing that real estate may be held in the partnership's name.

Uniform Residential Appraisal Report (URAR) (Form 1004) An appraisal form adopted for use by the U.S. Department of Housing and Urban Development, the Department of Veterans Affairs, and the Farmers Home Administration, in addition to the Freddie Mac and Fannie Mae.

Uniform Residential Landlord and Tenant Act (URLTA) A uniform act intended to provide some consistency in regulating the relationship of landlord and tenant in residential leases adopted in part or in full by a number of states.

Uniform Settlement Statement The standard RESPA Form or HUD-1 required to be given to the borrower, lender, and seller at or before settlement by the settlement agent in a transaction covered under the Real Estate Settlement Procedures Act; lenders must retain their copies for at least two years.

Uniform Simultaneous Death Act A statute adopted in most states designed to cover the situation where two joint tenants are killed in a common disaster.

Uniform Standards of Professional Appraisal Practice (USPAP) A set of ten standards developed in 1987, now updated annually, overseen by the Appraisal Standards Board of The Appraisal Foundation, that have been adopted by most state appraiser regulatory bodies.

Uniform Vendor and Purchaser Risk Act A law adopted in many states to determine which party bears the risk of loss if the property is damaged or destroyed before legal title passes to the vendee under a contract for sale.

unilateral contract A contract in which one party makes an obligation to perform without receiving in return any express promise of performance from the other party, such as an option in which the seller agrees to sell for a certain period of time at set terms, provided the buyer performs by paying the specified option price.

unimproved property Land without buildings, improvements, streets, and so on.

unincorporated association An assembly of people associated for some religious, scientific, fraternal, or recreational purpose not personally liable for debts incurred in the acquisition or leasing of real property used by the association, unless they specifically assume liability in writing.

unit A part of the property intended for any type of independent use and with an exit to a public street or corridor, commonly referring to the individual units in a condominium, exclusive of the common areas.

unit-in-place method An appraisal method of computing replacement cost; also called the segregated cost method, which uses prices for various building components, as installed, based on specific units of use such as square footage or cubic footage.

unit value Value or price related to a unit of measurement.

unity (joint tenancy) A concurrence of certain requirements; under common-law rules, the creation of a joint tenancy requires four unities: unity of interest, title, time, and possession.

universal agent A general agent; one authorized to act on behalf of another, such as an attorney-in-fact under a general power of attorney.

unjust enrichment The circumstances in which a person has received and retains money or goods that in fairness and justice belong to another.

unlawful detainer action A legal action that provides a method of evicting a tenant who is in default under the terms of the lease; a summary proceeding to recover possession of property.

unmarketable title A title to property that contains substantial defects such as undisclosed encroachments, building code violations, easements, or outstanding dower.

unrecorded deed A deed that is valid between grantor and grantee and anyone with notice of the ownership of the property.

unsecured Describes a debt instrument, such as a debenture, that is backed only by the debtor's promise to pay.

up-leg The replacement property purchased in a Section 1031, tax-deferred exchange; typically, the taxpayer trades up in an exchange.

upset price A minimum price set by a court in a judicial foreclosure, below which the property may not be sold by a court-appointed commissioner at public auction; the minimum price that can be accepted for the property after the court has had the property appraised.

upside-down A financial condition in which there is not enough equity in the property to pay the outstanding liens.

upzoning A change in zoning classification from a lower to a higher use.

urban renewal A process of upgrading deteriorated neighborhoods through clearance and redevelopment, rehabilitation, and the installation of new public improvements, or through modernization of existing ones, often funded with a combination of federal funds, local funds, or private monies.

urban sprawl The unplanned expansion of a municipality over a large geographical area.

usable area On a multitenancy floor, the gross area minus core space.

useful life That period of time over which an asset, such as a building, is expected to remain economically feasible to the owner.

use value The subjective value of a special-purpose property, designed to fit the particular requirements of the owner but that would have little or no use to another owner.

U.S. Geological Survey An agency within the U.S. Department of the Interior with responsibility for conservation, geological surveys, and mapping of lands within U.S. boundaries.

usufructuary right The right to the use, enjoyment, and profits of property belonging to another, such as an easement or profit a prendre.

usury The act of charging a rate of interest in excess of that permitted by law.

utilities The basic service system required by a developed area, such as telephone, electricity, water, and gas; utility easements are usually gross easements running on, over, or under the property.

utility value The value in use to an owner-user, which includes a value of amenities attaching to a property; also known as subjective value.

V

vacancy factor An allowance or discount for estimated vacancies (unrented units) in a rental project; the ratio between the number of vacant units and the total number of units in a specified project or area.

vacate To give up occupancy or surrender possession.

valid Legally sufficient or effective, such as a valid contract; a contract that must in all respects comply with the provisions of contract law.

valuable consideration The granting of some beneficial right, interest, or profit, or the suffering of some legal detriment or default by one party in return for the performance of another, usually as an inducement for a contract.

value The power of a good or service to command other goods in exchange for the present worth to typical users and investors of future benefits arising out of ownership of a property; the amount of money deemed to be the equivalent in worth of the subject property. The four essential elements of value are demand, utility, scarcity, and transferability (DUST). Cost does not equal value, nor does equity.

value added The anticipated increase in property value expected from fixing a condition causing accrued depreciation.

variable interest rate A modern approach to financing in which the lender is permitted to alter the interest rate under a loan, with a certain period of advance notice, based on an agreed basic index, such as the prime rate, thus increasing or decreasing monthly mortgage payments.

variance Permission obtained from governmental zoning authorities to build a structure or conduct a use that is expressly prohibited by the current zoning laws; an exception from the zoning laws.

vendee The purchaser of realty; the buyer; the buyer under contract for deed.

vendor The seller of realty; the seller under contract for deed.

vendor's lien The equitable lien of the grantor on the land conveyed in the amount of the unpaid purchase price.

venture capital Unsecured money directed toward an investment.

venue The place where the cause of action arose.

verify To confirm or substantiate by oath.

vested interest A present right, interest, or title to realty, which carries with it the existing right to convey, even though use of possession is postponed to some uncertain time in the future.

Veterans Administration (VA) loan A government-sponsored mortgage assistance program; eligible veterans and unremarried widows or widowers of veterans who died in service or from service-connected causes may obtain partially guaranteed loans for the purchase or construction of a house or to refinance existing mortgage debt. VA loans are administered by the Department of Veterans Affairs.

vicarious liability Liability created not because of a person's actions but because of the relationship between the liable person and other parties; for example, a real estate broker is vicariously liable for the acts of his or her salespeople while acting on behalf of the broker even if the broker did nothing to cause liability.

V

violation An act, deed, or condition contrary to the law or permissible use of real property.

void Having no legal force or binding effect; a nullity; not enforceable; a void contract need not be disaffirmed, nor can it be ratified.

voidable A contract that appears valid and enforceable on its face but is subject to rescission by one of the parties who acted under a disability.

voucher system In construction lending, a system of giving subcontractors a voucher that they may redeem with the construction lender in lieu of cash.

W

waiver To give up or surrender a right voluntarily.

walk-through A final inspection of a property just before closing to assure the buyer that the property has been vacated and requred repairs have been satisfactorily completed, and that otherwise, the property is in essentially the same condition that it was when the buyer made the offer.

warehouse A building used to store merchandise and other materials or equipment.

warehousing The holding of a number of mortgage loans held by a mortgage banker to be sold at a later date.

W

warranty A promise that certain stated facts are true; a guaranty by the seller, covering the title as well as the physical condition of the property; a breach of warranty action can result only in damages being awarded by a court, not rescission as with a misrepresentation.

warranty deed A deed in which the grantor fully warrants good clear title to the premises; also called a **general warranty deed**.

waste An improper use or abuse of property by a landowner who holds less than the fee ownership, such as a tenant, life tenant, mortgagor, or vendee.

wasteland Land that is deemed to be unfit for cultivation; unproductive, unimproved, barren land such as lava land.

wasting asset Property such as timber, an oil well, a quarry, or a mine, the substance of which is depleted through drilling and exploitation.

water In its natural state, water is real property, becoming personal property when it is severed from the realty and placed in containers; there are three classifications of water: *surface water; watercourse,* and *floodwater.*

watercourse A running stream of water following a regular course or channel and possessing a bed and banks.

waterfront property Real estate (improved or unimproved) abutting on a body of water such as a canal, lake, or ocean.

watershed The drainage area contributing to the water found in the abutting stream; the drainage basin.

water table The natural level at which water will be located, be it above or below the surface of the ground.

wear and tear The gradual physical deterioration of property, resulting from use, passage of time, and from weather.

wetlands Land areas where groundwater is at or near the surface of the ground for enough of each year so as to produce a wetland plant community; these lands are subject to many federal, state, and local controls, including environmental protection and zoning for special preservation and conservation.

widow's quarantine That period of time after the husband's death that a widow may remain in the house of her deceased husband without being charged rent.

wild deed A deed appearing in the chain of title in which the first party (grantor) has no recorded interest in the subject property.

will A written instrument disposing of probate property (tenancy in severalty or tenancy in common) upon the death of the maker (the testator).

withholding The process of holding back money earmarked for the payment of taxes.

without recourse A form of qualified endorsement relieving the maker of personal liability.

witness The act of signing one's name to a contract, deed, will, or other document for the purpose of attesting to its authenticity and proving its execution by testifying, if required.

workers' compensation law A state law requiring all employers to provide insurance coverage for their employees for work loss of employment due to work-related illness or injury.

working capital Liquid assets available for the conduct of daily business.

working drawings The final-stage drawings by an architect that show the lighting layout, electrical plugs, telephone outlets, and similar items, and that detail the precise method of construction.

work letter A detailed addition to a lease defining all improvement work to be done by the landlord for the tenant and specifying what work the tenant will perform at his or her own expense.

W

workout plan An attempt by a mortgagee to assist a mortgagor in default to work out a payment plan rather than proceed directly with a foreclosure.

wraparound mortgage A method of financing in which the new mortgage is placed in a secondary or subordinate position; the new mortgage includes both the unpaid principal balance of the first mortgage and whatever additional sums are advanced by the lender. Sometimes called an *all-inclusive loan,* an *overriding loan,* or an *overlapping loan.*

write-off
1. Clearing an asset off the accounting books, as with an uncollectable debt.
2. A tax deduction. (See **tax shelter**)

writ of execution A court order authorizing and directing an officer of the court (sheriff, police officer) to levy and sell property of the defendant to satisfy a judgment.

X A mark that may substitute for a signature in some cases, especially used by those who cannot write their names to indicate the intention to sign by marking an *X* in the place for signature.

x-ray fluorescent device (XRF) A handheld device used to detect the levels of lead in any underlying layers of lead-based paint.

yard
1. A unit of measurement equaling three feet.
2. The open, unoccupied space on the plot between the property line and the front, rear, or side wall of a building.

year-to-year tenancy A periodic tenancy in which the rent is reserved from year to year.

X–Z

yield The return on an investment or the amount of profit, stated as a percentage of the amount invested; the rate of return.

yield capitalization In the income approach to appraisal, a process whereby cash flows are projected over a holding period to include the proceeds of sale at the end of the holding period, and cash flow is discounted at a selected yield rate to estimate current value of the cash flows.

yield to maturity A method of financing repayment in which a borrower pays a certain percentage of actual funds borrowed each year (such as interest only) and pays the loan off in full at the end of its maturity.

zero lot line A term generally used to describe the positioning of a structure on a lot so that one side rests directly on the lot's boundary line.

zone condemnation The demolition and clearance of entire areas to make way for new construction, especially in slum clearance projects.

zoning The regulation of structures and uses of property within designated districts or zones; an exercise of police power upheld as long as they may reasonably protect the public health, safety, morals, and general welfare of an area.

zoning estoppel A rule that bars the government from enforcing a new downzoning ordinance against a landowner who had incurred substantial costs in reliance on the government's assurances that the landowner had met all the zoning requirements before the new downzoning took place.

ORGANIZATIONS

American Arbitration Association (AAA)

www.adr.org

A trade association with international participation offering education and training, publications, and the resolution of a wide range of disputes through mediation, arbitration, elections, and other out-of-court settlement techniques.

American Institute of Real Estate Appraisers (AIREA)

www.appraisalinstitute.org

A professional organization formerly affiliated with the National Association of REALTORS® and merged in 1991 with the Society of Real Estate Appraisers into the Appraisal Institute. Designations: Member, Appraisal Institute (MAI), Residential Member (RM).

American Land Development Association (ALDA)

A national trade association for real estate professionals involved in development of recreation and second homes by representing the interstate land development industry in matters related to land development. The mailing address is 1200 L Street, N.W., Washington, D.C. 20005; (202) 371-6700.

American Land Title Association (ALTA)
www.alta.org

An association of land title companies whose collective objectives include using uniform ALTA title insurance forms to provide standardization in the transfer of ownership within the free enterprise system. ALTA members provide information and education to consumers and government regulators working with legislation affecting the land title evidencing industry, and to its own members. ALTA members may provide abstracts, issue title insurance, or act as agents for title insurance underwriting companies.

American National Standards Institute (ANSI)
www.ansi.org

A private, nonprofit organization (501[c]3) that administers and coordinates the U.S. voluntary standardization and conformity assessment system. ANSI promotes and facilitates voluntary consensus standards and conformity assessment systems.

American Society for Industrial Security (ASIS)
www.asisonline.org

A professional association of industrial security personnel. Certification programs: Certified Protection Professional (CPP), Professional Certified

Investigator (PCI), and Physical Security Professional (PSP).

American Society of Appraisers (ASA)

www.appraisers.org

A professional organization of appraisers engaged in the appraisal of both real and personal property. Designations: Accredited Member (AM), Accredited Senior Appraiser (ASA).

American Society of Farm Managers and Rural Appraisers

www.asfmra.org

A professional association representing professionals in financial analysis, valuation, and management of agricultural and rural resources, including farm management. Certifications: Accredited Farm Manager (AFM), Accredited Rural Appraiser (ARA), Real Property Review Appraiser (RPRA), Accredited Agricultural Consultant (AAC).

American Society of Home Inspectors (ASHI)

www.ashi.org

A professional organization of home inspectors from the United States and Canada, meeting the needs of its membership by building public awareness of home inspections and promoting excellence and exemplary practice within the profession under ASHI's Standards of Practice and Code of Ethics.

American Society of Real Estate Counselors (ASREC)

www.cre.org

A professional organization, affiliated with the National Association of REALTORS®, composed of individuals who serve clients on a fee basis. Designation: Counselor of Real Estate (CRE).

America's Community Bankers

www.acbankers.org

A trade association representing community banks of all charter types whose members provide financial services to their communities and customers. It implements a broad range of advocacy and progressive, entrepreneurial, and service-oriented strategies. Offers an Executive MBA in Community Banking in cooperation with Fairfield University in Connecticut.

Appraisal Foundation

www.appraisalfoundation.org

A self-regulated organization created for the purpose of developing appraisal standards and appraiser qualifications by the Financial Institutions Reform, Recovery and Enforcement Act of 1989 (FIRREA). The five-member Appraiser Qualification Board approves the education, experience, and testing requirements for state certification of appraisers. The Appraisal Standards Board establishes minimum standards for appraisers.

Appraisal Institute
www.appraisalinstitute.org

A professional real estate organization formed as a result of the merger of the American Institute of Real Estate Appraisers and the Society of Real Estate Appraisers. Designations: Member, Appraisal Institute (MAI) and Senior Residential Appraiser (SRA).

Appraisal Institute of Canada (AIC)
www.aicanada.ca

A Canadian, self-regulating body protecting the public interest by maintaining high standards, practices, and professional conduct in real estate appraisal. Designations: Canadian Residential Appraiser (CRA); Accredited Appraiser Canadian Institute (AACI); Professional Appraiser (P.App).

Association of Real Estate License Law Officials (ARELLO)
www.arello.org

A professional organization of real estate commissioners and real estate administrators from all 50 states, three Canadian provinces, Guam, Puerto Rico, and the Virgin Islands. A joint committee of ARELLO and the National Association of REALTORS® (NAR) has drafted several model license laws since the early 1960s, since adopted by the various states.

Building Owners and Managers Association (BOMA)

www.boma.org

An international professional organization of 100 North American and nine overseas affiliates and the primary information source for office building development, leasing, building operating costs, energy consumption patterns, local and national building codes, legislation, occupancy statistics, and technological developments. Its members are building owners, managers, developers, leasing professionals, medical office building managers, corporate facility managers, asset managers, and the providers of the products and services needed to operate commercial properties.

Building Owners and Managers Institute (BOMI)

www.bomi-edu.org

The educational arm of BOMA. Designations: Real Property Administrator (RPA), Facilities Management Administrator (FMA), Systems Maintenance Administrator (SMA), and Systems Maintenance Technician (SMT).

Bureau of Land Management (BLM)

www.blm.gov

An agency within the U.S. Department of the Interior; administers 261 million surface acres of America's public lands, located primarily in 12 western states. The BLM sustains the health, diversity, and productivity of the public lands for the use and enjoyment of present and future generations.

Chinese American Real Estate Professional Association (CAREPA)

www.carepa.org

A national association of Chinese American real estate professionals seeking to further home ownership in the Chinese American communities and to conduct a high, ethical real estate practice in Chinese American communities.

ChoiceTrust by ChoicePoint

www.choicetrust.com

A for-profit company that compiles records from local, state, and federal government agencies into searchable databases to provide information about a variety of topics, including those used by the insurance industry. The CLUE (Comprehensive Loss Underwriting Exchange) is a database of consumer claims created by ChoicePoint that the majority of insurance companies access when underwriting or rating an insurance policy. C.L.U.E. Personal Property reports contain up to five years of personal property claims matching the search criteria submitted by the inquiring insurance company. CLUE must comply with Fair Credit Reporting Act (FCRA) disclosure requirements.

Commercial Investment Real Estate Institute

www.ccim.com

A professional organization of real estate practitioners specializing in commercial real estate, affiliated with the National Association of REALTORS®. Designation: Certified Commercial Investment Member (CCIM).

Community Associations Institute (CAI)

www.caionline.org

A not-for-profit research and educational organization offering education for creating, financing, operating, and maintaining the common facilities and services in condominiums, townhouse projects, planned unit developments, and open-space communities. Certification (with National Board of Certification for Community Association Mangers (NBC-CAM) the Certified Manager of Community Associations (CMCA)). Designations: Association Management Specialist (AMS); Professional Community Association Manager (PCAM); Accredited Association Management Company (AAMC); Large-Scale Manager (LSM); Reserve Specialist (RS); Community Insurance and Risk Management Specialist (CIRMS); College of Community Association Lawyers (CCAL).

Council of Real Estate Brokerage Managers

www.crb.com

A not-for-profit affiliate of the National Association of REALTORS® offering training and education to brokers and owners of real estate companies. Designation: Certified Real Estate Brokerage Manager (CRB).

Department of Housing and Urban Development

www.hud.gov

A U.S. government agency created in 1965, consolidating older federal agencies to administer federal housing and community programs and urban development, and fair housing laws. HUD plays a major role in fostering home ownership by underwriting loans for lower- and moderate-income families through its mortgage insurance programs such as the Federal Housing Administration (FHA), Ginnie Mae, and the Community Development Block Grant (CDBG). Designations: Area Management Brokers (AMBs).

Environmental Protection Agency (EPA)

www.epa.gov

A federal agency created in 1970 to coordinate government action on behalf of the environment by a variety of research, monitoring, standard setting, and enforcement activities. The EPA coordinates and supports research and antipollution activities by state and local governments, private and public groups, individuals, and educational institutions. It also monitors the environmental impact of other Federal agencies and is specifically charged with making public its written comments on environmental impact statements (EIS).

Fair Isaac & Company (FICO)
www.myfico.com

A for-profit company best known for developing the FICO scores as a method of determining the likelihood that credit users will pay their bills, by condensing a borrower's credit history into a single number. Lenders use FICO scores, computed by data provided by each of the three credit bureaus–Experian, Trans Union, and Equifax—to determine loan availability.

Fannie Mae
www.fanniemae.com

A private, shareholder-owned company since 1968 actively traded on the N.Y. Stock Exchange and other exchanges; created by the Federal government in 1938 to expand the flow of mortgage money by creating a secondary market for FHA-insured mortgages. Today, Fannie Mae operates under a congressional charter that directs it to increase the availability and affordability of home ownership for low-, moderate-, and middle-income Americans.

Farm and Land Institute

An organization that is now the REALTORS® Land Institute (RLI).

Farmer's Home Administration (FmHA)

Formerly an agency of the U.S. Department of Agriculture (USDA) that provided direct and guaranteed credit to family-sized farmers who were denied credit by a commercial lender. The 1994 USDA reorganization transferred FmHA's farm loan programs to the newly formed Farm Service Agency (FSA).

Farm Credit Administration (FCA)
www.fca.gov

An independent agency in the U.S. government responsible for regulating and examining the banks, associations, and so on that collectively comprise the Farm Credit System, including the Federal Agricultural Mortgage Corporation (Farmer Mac) in order to promote a safe, sound, and dependable source of credit and related services for agriculture and rural America.

Farm Credit System Banks (FCSB)
www.farmcredit-ffcb.com

A nationwide network of borrower-owned lending institutions and affiliated service entities that lend to agricultural producers, cooperatives, and certain farm-related business. Unlike commercial banks, the System banks do not accept deposits and provide financial and human resources necessary to underwrite, distribute, and maintain a primary and secondary market in Farm Credit Debt Securities.

Farm Service Agency
www.fsa.usda.gov

An agency created by the merger of several other agencies under the USDA responsible for administering farm income-support programs, conservation cost-sharing programs, and farm loan programs through field service centers located throughout the United States. Each state FSA is led by a state executive director (SED).

Federal Agricultural Mortgage Corporation (Farmer Mac)
www.farmermac.com

A government-sponsored, stockholder-owned, publicly traded company regulated by the Farm Credit Administration (FCA) that provides a secondary market for first mortgage agricultural and rural housing real estate loans. Working with the USDA, Farmer Mac purchases loans from agricultural lenders, sells instruments backed by these loans, and seeks to maintain a sufficient liquidity reserve, and surplus funds with appropriate interest-rate risk.

Federal Deposit Insurance Corporation (FDIC)
www.fdic.gov

An independent agency of the federal government that seeks to promote public confidence in the U.S. financial system by insuring deposits in banks and thrift institutions for up to $100,000 by identifying, monitoring, and addressing risks to the deposit insurance funds and by limiting the effect on the economy and the financial system when a bank or thrift institution fails.

Federal Emergency Management Agency (FEMA)
www.fema.gov

A former independent agency that became part of the Department of Homeland Security in March 2003. Responsible for disaster mitigation, preparedness, response, and recovery planning.

Federal Financial Institutions Examinations Council (FFIEC)
www.ffiec.gov

An interagency of federal regulatory agency representatives organized to promote uniformity among commercial banks, savings associations, and credit unions by prescribing uniform principles, standards, and report forms for the federal examination of financial institutions by the Board of Governors of the Federal Reserve System (FRB), the Federal Deposit Insurance Corporation (FDIC), the National Credit Union Administration (NCUA), the Office of the Comptroller of the Currency (OCC), and the Office of Thrift Supervision (OTS).

Federal Housing Finance Board (FHFB)
www.fhfb.gov

The Federal Housing Finance Board regulates the 12 FHL Banks created in 1932 to improve the supply of funds to local lenders that, in turn, finance loans for home mortgages. The board ensures the safety and soundness of the Federal Home Loan Banks, their access to the capital markets, and the accomplishment of their congressionally defined housing finance mission.

Federal Land Bank (FLB)

Twelve banks established in 1916 to provide long-term mortgage credit to farmers and ranchers, and later to rural homebuyers, but by 1988, the last merged to form Farm Credit Banks.

Federal Savings and Loan Insurance Corporation (FSLIC)

Formerly, a federal institution responsible for insuring the deposits at savings and loan institutions in a manner similar to that of the Federal Deposit Insurance Corporation (FDIC) by insuring deposits for commercial banks. Its functions were assumed by the Federal Deposit Insurance Corporation (FDIC) in the 1980s.

Federal Trade Commission (FTC)

www.ftc.gov

A federal agency created to investigate and eliminate unfair and deceptive trade practices or unfair methods of competition, and false and misleading advertising in interstate commerce. The FTC has very broad antitrust and consumer protection authority.

Freddie Mac

www.freddiemac.com

A quasi-governmental, federally chartered corporation that is one of America's largest buyers of home mortgages from insured depository institutions and HUD-approved mortgage bankers, including commercial banks, mortgage banks, savings institutions, and credit unions. Freddie Mac is supervised by the U.S. Department of Housing and Urban Development (HUD).

General Services Administration (GSA)

www.gsa.gov

An independent, central management federal agency that sets federal policy for procurement and real property management and information resources management, i.e., it manages, leases, and sells buildings belonging to the U.S. Government. The GSA supplies products and communications for U.S. government offices, provides transportation and housing to federal employees, and develops government-wide cost-minimizing policies.

Ginnie Mae

www.ginniemae.gov

A government corporation that guarantees federally insured or guaranteed loans; mainly loans insured by the Federal Housing Administration (FHA) or guaranteed by the Department of Veterans Affairs (VA). Other guarantors or issuers of loans eligible as collateral for Ginnie Mae Mortgage Backed Securities (MBS) include the Department of Agriculture's Rural Housing Service (RHS) and the Department of Housing and Urban Development's Office of Public and Indian Housing (PIH).

Institute of Real Estate Management (IREM)
www.irem.org

A professional real estate management association serving both multifamily and commercial real estate sectors, an affiliate of the National Association of REALTORS®. Designations: Certified Property Manager® (CPM), the Accredited Residential Manager (ARM), and the Accredited Management Organization (AMO).

Internal Revenue Service (IRS)
www.irs.gov

A bureau of the Department of the Treasury whose role is to help taxpayers understand the tax laws passed by Congress, while ensuring that everyone pays his or her fair share of the taxes.

International Council of Shopping Centers (ICSC)
www.icsc.org

A global trade organization of shopping center owners, managers, and major tenants that functions as a medium for the interchange of information about shopping center practices and operations. Designations: Certified Shopping

Center Manager (CSM); Certified Leasing Special-
ist (CLS); Certified Marketing Director (CMD);
Senior Level Certified Shopping Center Manager
(SCSM); Accredited Shopping Center Manager
(ASM); Senior Level Certified Shopping Center
Marketing Director (SCMD); Accredited Market-
ing Director (AMD).

International Facility Management Association (IFMA)
www.ifma.org

An international, professional organization for
facility management that conducts research, provides educational programs, and recognizes facility management degree and certificate programs.
Designation: Certified Facility Management (CFM).

International Real Estate Federation (IREF)
www.fiabci.com

An international association of real estate professionals who provide essential commercial information about local markets to professional real
estate associations. Designation Certified International Property Specialist (CIPS).

Manufactured Housing Institute (MHI)
www.mfghome.org

A national trade organization serving all segments
of the factory-built housing industry by providing
industry research, promotion, education, and government relations programs.

National Affordable Housing Management Association (NAHMA)

www.nahma.org

A nonprofit organization for affordable housing advocating on behalf of multifamily property owners and managers providing quality affordable housing. The membership—multifamily property owners, managers, and industry stakeholders—support legislative and regulatory policies that promote the development and preservation of decent and safe housing by providing technical education and information between government and industry. Designations: Certified Professional of Occupancy (CPO); Housing Credit Certified Professional (HCCP).

National Apartment Association (NAA)

www.naahq.org

A professional organization serving the interests of multifamily housing owners, managers, developers, and suppliers and provides education and training opportunities for both multisite managers and on-site staff. NAA works with the National Multi Housing Council to monitor legislation and regulations at the federal level. Designations: Certified Apartment Property Supervision (CAPS); Certified Apartment Manager (CAM); Certified Apartment Maintenance Technician (CAMT); National Apartment Leasing Professional (NALP); Certified Apartment Supplier (CAS).

National Association of Exclusive Buyer Brokers (NAEBA)

www.naeba.org

An independent alliance of real estate professionals who provide client-level services only to buyer clients and whose real estate companies do not accept seller-property listings.

National Association of Hispanic Real Estate Professionals (NAHREP)

www.nahrep.org

A national trade association of Hispanic real estate professionals or those who work with Hispanics or who want to work with Spanish-speaking consumers.

National Association of Home Builders (NAHB)

www.nahb.org

A trade association consisting of more than 205,000 residential homebuilding and remodeling industry members. Designations: Certified New Home Sales Professional (CSP); Registered in Apartment Management (RAM); Certified Leasing Professional (CLP); plus many others.

National Association of Housing and Redevelopment Officials (NAHRO)

www.nahro.org

A professional organization of officials who administer HUD programs such as Public Housing,

Section 8, and others to advocate for providing adequate and affordable housing for all Americans, including those with low and moderate income.

National Association of Independent Fee Appraisers (NAIFA)

www.naifa.com

A professional association of appraisers seeking to raise standards in the appraisal industry and to gain recognition for its members. Designations: Independent Fee Affiliate (IFA); Independent Fee Affiliate Senior (IFAS); Independent Fee Affiliate Counselor (IFAC).

National Association of Industrial and Office Parks (NAIOP)

www.naiop.org

A national trade association representing the interests of developers and owners of industrial, office, and related commercial real estate throughout North America through communication, networking, and business opportunities for all real estate related professionals.

National Association of Master Appraisers (NAMA)

www.masterappraisers.org

A professional association of appraisers formed by real estate educators to improve the practice of real estate appraising through mandatory specific education. Designations: Master Residential Appraiser (MRA), Master Farm and Land Appraiser (MFLA), Master Senior Appraiser (MSA); Certified Appraisal Organization (CAO).

National Association of Real Estate Appraisers (NAREA)

www.iami.org/narea.cfm

One of the largest professional associations of appraisers. Designations: Certified Real Estate Appraiser (CREA), Certified Commercial Real Estate Appraiser (CCREA).

National Association of Real Estate Brokers (NAREB)

www.nareb.com

The oldest trade association of minority professionals in the real estate industry, consisting of local boards in principal cities throughout the U.S.; the members are called Realtists. The organization is open to any real estate licensee committed to achieving the ideal of the Realtist organization: democracy in housing.

National Association of Real Estate Investment Trusts (NAREIT)

www.nareit.org

A professional organization representing real estate investment trusts (REITs) and publicly traded real estate companies worldwide and whose members are REITs, academics, investors, industry professionals, and other businesses that own, operate, and finance income-producing real estate, and firms and individuals who advise, study, and service these businesses.

National Association of Real Estate License Law Officials

See *Association of Real Estate License Law Officials (ARELLO).*

National Association of REALTORS® (NAR)
www.realtor.com

The largest real estate organization in the world with more than one million members including REALTORS® and REALTOR® ASSOCIATES® representing all branches of the real estate industry. The national organization functions through local boards and state associations. Active brokers admitted to membership in state and local NAR boards are allowed to use the trademark REAL-TOR®. Salespeople are admitted on a REALTOR® ASSOCIATES® active status. NAR members subscribe to a strict Code of Ethics.

National professional organizations directly affiliated with NAR include the following: REALTORS® National Marketing Institute (formerly known as the National Institute of Real Estate Brokers, or NIREB); Commercial Investment Real Estate Institute (CIREI); Society of Industrial and Office REAL-TORS® (SIOR); Institute of Real Estate Management

(IREM); REALTOR® Land Institute (RLI); Real Estate Securities and Syndication Institute (RESSI); American Society of Real Estate Counselors (ASREC); Women's Council of REALTORS® (WCR); and the American Chapter of the International Real Estate Federation.

National Association of Residential Property Managers (NARPM)

www.narpm.org

A professional association of real estate professionals who specialize in managing single-family and small residential properties. Designations: Professional Property Manager (PPM); Master Property Manager (MPM).

National Association of Review Appraisers and Mortgage Underwriters (NARA/MU)

www.iami.org

A nonprofit, national organization whose members review appraisals and underwrite mortgages; one of the largest "consumers" of appraisals in the nation. Designations: Certified Review Appraiser (CRA) and Registered Mortgage Underwriter (RMU).

National Association of Securities Dealers (NASD)

www.nasd.com

A nonprofit, self-regulatory organization registered with the Securities Exchange Commission that governs the practices of broker-dealer firms in the OTC market with federal authority to discipline securities firms and individuals in the securities industry who violate the rules by fining, suspending, or expelling them from the industry. The NASD has authority over securities salespeople such as those selling real estate securities, resort condominiums with rental pools and tax shelters in programs providing a direct "pass-through" of tax benefits, and limited partnerships and REITs, but not stock in ordinary corporations. Licenses: Limited Representative License, Limited Principal's License.

National Investment Center for the Seniors Housing and Care Industries (NIC)
www.nic.org

An independent, nonprofit organization facilitating efficient capital formation for the seniors' housing and care industries through research, networking, and providing business and financial information to lenders, investors, developers/ operators, and others interested in meeting the housing and healthcare needs of senior citizens in the U.S.

Office of Equal Opportunity (OEO)
www.doi.gov/diversity

The federal agency under the direction of the Secretary of the Department of Housing and Urban

Development that is in charge of administering the federal Fair Housing Act.

Office of Interstate Land Sales Registration (OILSR)
www.hud.gov/offices/hsg/sfh/ils/ils1008.cfm

A federal agency, part of HUD, that regulates interstate land sales to prevent abuse, such as fraud and misrepresentation, perpetrated on the public in the promotion and sale of recreational property across state lines.

Office of the Comptroller of the Currency (OCC)
www.occ.treas.gov

A federal agency within the U.S. Treasury Department that charters, regulates, and examines approximately 2600 national banks, 66 federal branches, and agencies of foreign banks in the United States.

REALTORS® Institute
www.realtor.org

A series of classes leading to the professional designation Graduate, REALTORS® Institute (GRI), which may be earned by any member of a state-affiliated Board of REALTORS® who successfully completes prescribed courses approved by the state Board of REALTORS®. State associations generally sponsor the GRI courses covering law, finance, investment, appraisal, office management, and salesmanship.

Real Estate Brokerage Council

A council affiliated with NAR's REALTORS® National Marketing Institute (RNMI), whose goal is to improve standards and professionalism in real estate brokerage management. Designation: Certified Real Estate Brokerage Manager (CRB).

Real Estate Educators Association (REEA)
www.reea.org

A professional organization established by and for real estate educators, including individuals and institutions. REEA is international in scope and represents every aspect of real estate education from degree programs and proprietary schools to publishers. Designation: Distinguished Real Estate Instructor (DREI).

REALTORS® Land Institute (RLI)
www.rliland.com

A professional organization formerly known as the Farm & Land Institute, now an affiliate of the National Association of REALTORS® (NAR) focused on land brokerage transactions of five specialized types: farms and ranches, undeveloped tracts of land, transitional and development land, subdivision and wholesaling of lots, and site selection and assemblage of land parcels. Individual members frequently engage in other land specialties such as agribusiness, appraisal, consulting, and management. Designation: Accredited Land Consultant (ALC).

REALTORS® National Marketing Institute (RNMI)
www.crb.com

A professional organization affiliated with the National Association of REALTORS®, dedicated to education in areas of marketing, income property investment analysis, and office management. Designations: Certified Commercial and Investment Member (CCIM), Certified Residential Broker (CRB), Certified Residential Salesperson (CRS).

Residential Sales Council (RS)
www.crs.com

A council of residential specialists affiliated with NAR's REALTORS® National Marketing Institute (RNMI) that focuses on listing and marketing skills for residential real estate agents. Designation: Certified Residential Specialist (CRS).

Resolution Trust Corporation (RTC)

A now defunct agency created as a part of FIRREA for the purpose of receiving the assets of failed savings associations and disposing of repossessed property through direct sales and auction sales.

Rural Housing Service
www.rurdev.usda.gov/rhs

A service provided by the U.S. Department of Agriculture to assist rural homeowners to buy, repair, or renovate homes by making financing available to the elderly, disabled, and low-income families through rent subsidies and several loan, grant, and guarantee programs.

Small Business Administration (SBA)
www.sba.gov

An independent federal agency in the executive branch created to provide management and financial assistance to small businesses, primarily by either making loans directly or guaranteeing loans through financial institutions. The loans may be used for working capital, machinery and equipment, acquisition of real estate, and expansion.

Society of Industrial and Office REALTORS® (SIOR)
www.sior.com

A professional organization affiliated with the National Association of REALTORS® (NAR), whose members specialize in the marketing of industrial and office properties. Designations: Specialist, Industrial and/or Office Real Estate (SIOR).

Society of Real Estate Appraisers (SREA)
www.nareb.com

An international organization of professional real estate appraisers combined with the American Institute of Real Estate Appraisers to form the Appraisal Institute. The following designations may be retained by members: Senior Residential Appraiser (SRA), Senior Real Property Appraiser (SRPA), Senior Real Estate Analyst (SREA). Designations awarded by the Appraisal Institute are MAI and SRA. (See **Appraisal Institute**).

Urban Land Institute (ULI)
www.uli.org

An independent, nonprofit research and educational organization comprised of individuals working in private enterprise and public service to improve the quality and standards of land use and real estate development. Certifications: Real Estate Development Certification; Real Estate Development Financing Certification.

Women's Council of REALTORS® (WCR)
www.wcr.org

An organization originally founded by women for women within the National Association of REALTORS® and whose purpose today is to expand its members' knowledge of the real estate business and provide an opportunity for sharing experiences and exchanging information.

DESIGNATIONS

Note: Terms in italics denote organizations listed in Appendix A.

AAC	Accredited Agricultural Consultant, see *American Society of Farm Managers and Rural Appraisers*
AACI	Accredited Appraiser Canadian Institute, see *Appraisal Institute of Canada (AIC)*
AAMC	Accredited Association Management Company, see *Community Associations Institute (CAI)*
AFM	Accredited Farm Manager, see *American Society of Farm Managers and Rural Appraisers*
ALC	Accredited Land Consultant, see *REALTORS® Land Institute*
AM	Accredited Member, see *American Society of Appraisers (ASA)*

AMBs	Area Management Brokers, see *Department of Housing and Urban Development (HUD)*
AMD	Accredited Marketing Director, see *International Council of Shopping Centers (ICSC)*
AMO	Accredited Management Organization, see *Institute of Real Estate Management (IREM)*
AMS	Association Management Specialist, see *Community Associations Institute (CAI)*
ARA	Accredited Rural Appraiser, see *American Society of Farm Managers and Rural Appraisers*
ARM	Accredited Residential Manager, see *Institute of Real Estate Management (IREM)*
ASA	Accredited Senior Appraiser, see *American Society of Appraisers (ASA)*
ASM	Accredited Shopping Center Manager, see *International Council of Shopping Centers (ICSC)*

CAM	Certified Apartment Manager, see *National Apartment Association (NAA)*
CAMT	Certified Apartment Maintenance Technician, see *National Apartment Association (NAA)*
CAO	Certified Appraisal Organization, see *National Association of Master Appraisers (NAMA)*
CAPS	Certified Apartment Property Supervision, see *National Apartment Association (NAA)*
CAS	Certified Apartment Supplier, see *National Apartment Association (NAA)*
CCAL	College of Community Association Lawyers, see *Community Associations Institute (CAI)*
CCIM	Certified Commercial Investment Member, see *Commercial Investment Real Estate Institute; REALTORS® National Marketing Institute (RNMI)*
CCREA	Certified Commercial Real Estate Appraiser, see *National Association of Real Estate Appraisers (NAREA)*

CFM	Certified Facility Management, see *International Facility Management Association (IFMA)*
CIPS	Certified International Property Specialist, see *International Real Estate Federation*
CIRMS	Community Insurance and Risk Management Specialist, see *Community Associations Institute (CAI)*
CLP	Certified Leasing Professional, see *National Association of Home Builders (NAHB)*
CLS	Certified Leasing Specialist, see *International Council of Shopping Centers (ICSC)*
CMCA	Certified Manager of Community Associations, see *Community Associations Institute (CAI)*
CMD	Certified Marketing Director, see *International Council of Shopping Centers (ICSC)*
CPM	Certified Property Manager ®, see *Institute of Real Estate Management (IREM)*

CPO	Certified Professional of Occupancy, see *National Affordable Housing Management Association (NAHMA)*
CPP	Certified Protection Professional, see *American Society for Industrial Security (ASIS)*
CRA	Canadian Residential Appraiser, see *Appraisal Institute of Canada (AIC)*
CRA	Certified Review Appraiser, see *National Association of Review Appraisers and Mortgage Underwriters*
CRB	Certified Real Estate Brokerage Manager, see *Real Estate Brokerage Council*
CRB	Certified Real Estate Brokerage Manager, see *Council of Real Estate Brokerage Managers*
CRB	Certified Residential Broker, see REALTORS® *National Marketing Institute (RNMI)*
CRE	Counselor of Real Estate, see *American Society of Real Estate Counselors (ASREC)*

CREA   Certified Real Estate Appraiser, see *National Association of Real Estate Appraisers (NAREA)*

CRS   Certified Residential Salesperson, see *REALTORS® National Marketing Institute (RNMI)*

CRS   Certified Residential Specialist, see *Council of Residential Specialists (CRS)*

CSM   Certified Shopping Center Manager, see *International Council of Shopping Centers (ICSC)*

CSP   Certified New Home Sales Professional, see *National Association of Home Builders (NAHB)*

DREI   Distinguished Real Estate Instructor, see *Real Estate Educators Association (REEA)*

FMA   Facilities Management Administrator, see *Building Owners and Managers Institute (BOMI)*

GRI   Graduate, REALTORS® Institute, see *REALTORS® Institute; National Association of REALTORS®*

HCCP	Housing Credit Certified Professional, see *National Affordable Housing Management Association (NAHMA)*
IFA	Independent Fee Affiliate, see *National Association of Independent Fee Appraisers (NAIFA)*
IFAC	Independent Fee Affiliate Counselor, see *National Association of Independent Fee Appraisers (NAIFA)*
IFAS	Independent Fee Affiliate Senior, see *National Association of Independent Fee Appraisers (NAIFA)*
Limited Principal's License	See *National Association of Securities Dealers (NASD)*
Limited Representative License	See *National Association of Securities Dealers (NASD)*
LSM	Large-Scale Manager, see *Community Associations Institute (CAI)*
MAI	Member, Appraisal Institute, see *Appraisal Institute; American Institute of Real Estate Appraisers (AIREA)*

MFLA	Master Farm and Land Appraiser, see *National Association of Master Appraisers (NAMA)*
MPM	Master Property Manager, see *National Association of Residential Property Managers (NARPM)*
MRA	Master Residential Appraiser, see *National Association of Master Appraisers (NAMA)*
MSA	Master Senior Appraiser, see *National Association of Master Appraisers (NAMA)*
NALP	National Apartment Leasing Professional, see *National Apartment Association (NAA)*
P.App	Professional Appraiser, see *Appraisal Institute of Canada (AIC)*
PCAM	Professional Community Association Manager, see *Community Associations Institute (CAI)*
PCI	Professional Certified Investigator, see *American Society for Industrial Security (ASIS)*

PPM	Professional Property Manager, see *National Association of Residential Property Managers (NARPM)*
PSP	Physical Security Professional, see *American Society for Industrial Security (ASIS)*
RAM	Registered in Apartment Management, see *National Association of Home Builders (NAHB)*
Real Estate Development Certification	See *Urban Land Institute (ULI)*
Real Estate Development Financing Certification	See *Urban Land Institute (ULI)*
Realtist	See *National Association of Real Estate Brokers (NAREB)*
REALTOR®	See *National Association of REALTORS® (NAR)*
RM	Residential Member, see *American Institute of Real Estate Appraisers (AIREA)*

RMU   Registered Mortgage Under-
                   writer, see *National Association
                   of Review Appraisers and Mort-
                   gage Underwriters*

RPA   Real Property Administrator, see
                   *Building Owners and Manag-
                   ers Institute (BOMI)*

RPRA   Real Property Review Appraiser,
                   see *American Society of Farm
                   Managers and Rural Appraisers*

RS   Reserve Specialist, see *Commu-
                   nity Associations Institute (CAI)*

SCSM   Senior Level Certified Shopping
                   Center Manager, see *Interna-
                   tional Council of Shopping Cen-
                   ters (ICSC)*

SCMD   Senior Level Certified Shopping
                   Center Marketing Director, *see
                   International Council of Shop-
                   ping Centers (ICSC)*

SIOR   Specialist, Industrial and/or
                   Office Real Estate, see *Society of
                   Industrial and Office REALTORS®
                   (SIOR)*

SMA   Systems Maintenance Adminis-
                   trator, see *Building Owners and
                   Managers Institute (BOMI)*

SMT	Systems Maintenance Technician, see *Building Owners and Managers Institute (BOMI)*
SRA	Senior Residential Appraiser, see *Society of Real Estate Appraisers (SREA)*
SRA	Senior Residential Appraiser, see *Appraisal Institute*
SREA	Senior Real Estate Analyst, see *Society of Real Estate Appraisers (SREA)*
SRPA	Senior Real Property Appraiser, see *Society of Real Estate Appraisers (SREA)*

ABBREVIATIONS OF TERMS

A	
a/c	air-conditioning
ac; A	acre
ACM	asbestos-containing material
ACRS	accelerated-cost recovery system
ADR	asset-depreciation range system
ADS	alternative depreciation system
ADT	average daily traffic
AFD	agreement for deed
AFR	applicable federal rate
AITD	all-inclusive trust deed
aka	also known as
ALJ	administrative law judge
AMB	area management broker
APR	annual percentage rate

ARM	adjustable-rate mortgage
ATCF	after-tax cash flow

B

BA	bathroom
BD	bedroom
BFP	bona fide purchaser
BID	business improvement district
BHC	bank holding company
BIC	broker-in-charge
BIF	bank insurance fund
BRI	building-related illness
BTU	British thermal unit

C

CAM	common area maintenance
Cap	capitalization
CB	carry back
CBD	central business district
CBS	concrete block and stucco
CCD	Census County Division
CC&Rs	covenants, conditions, and restrictions

CD	certificate of deposit
CF	cash flow
CFC	chlorofluorocarbons
CFD	contract for deed
CLO	computerized loan origination
CLTV	combined loan to value
CMA	comparative market analysis
CMO	collateralized mortgage obligation
Co.	company
CO	carbon monoxide
COB	close of business
COC	certificate of completion
COF	cost of funds
CON	connected (sewer)
COCR	cash on cash return
COO	certificate of occupancy
CPA	Certified Public Accountant
CPI	consumer price index
CRA	credit rating agency
CRE	creative real estate

CRV	certificate of reasonable value
CSM	certified survey map
CT	conveyance tax
CTL	cash-to-loan ratio
CZC	comprehensive zoning code

D

DCF	discounted cash flow
DCR	debt coverage ratio
d/b/a	"doing business as"
DBH	diameter breast-high
DCRR	discounted rate of return
DLUM	detailed land-use map
DOG	bad investment
DOS	due-on-sale clause
DOT	deed of trust; Department of Transportation
DP	down payment
DPC	debt previously contracted
DR	dining room
DRM	direct reduction mortgage

DSCR	debt service coverage ratio
DT	depth tables

E

EA	exclusive agency
EBA	exclusive buyer agent
EC	extended coverage
EIFS	exterior insulation and finish systems
EIS	environmental impact statement
EM	earnest money deposit
EMAC	enclosed mall air-conditioned
E&O	errors & omissions insurance
ERA	environmental risk audits
ESA	environmental site assessment
ESOP	employee stock ownership plan

F

FAR	floor area ratio
FB	full bath
FFE	furniture, fixture, and equipment
FH	flood hazard
FICB	federal intermediate credit banks

FIFO	first in, first out (accounting)
FLB	federal land bank
FLIP®	Flexible Loan Insurance Program
FMR	fair market rent
FMV	fair market value
FP	file plan
FRM	fixed-rate mortgage
FS	fee simple
FRBO	for rent by owner
FSBO	for sale by owner

G

GBA	gross buildable area
GCR	guest-car ratio
GEM	growing equity mortgage
GIT	gross income tax
GLA	gross leasable area; gross living area
GMC	guaranteed mortgage certificate
GP	general plan
GPARM	graduated payment adjustable-rate mortgage

GPM	graduated payment mortgage
GRM	gross rent multiplier
GSP	guaranteed sales program

H

HBU	highest and best use
HELOC	home equity line of credit
HEPA	high-efficiency particulate acquisition
HML	hard money lender
HOA	homeowners' association
HOW	Homeowners' Warranty Program
HMIS	hazardous material identification system
HRS	hazard rank system
HSF	heated square feet
HUD	U.S. Department of Housing and Urban Development
HVAC	heating, ventilation, and air-conditioning

I–K

| **IFA** | independent fee appraiser |
| **IRA** | individual retirement account |

IRC	Internal Revenue Code
IRR	internal rate of return
IRS	Internal Revenue Service
IS	information systems
IT	information technology
J/T	joint tenant
Kit	kitchen

L	
L	leasehold
L#	liber number (book number)
LA	living area
LR	living room
LAL	limit on artificial accounting losses
LDD	local development district
LH	leasehold
LHA	local housing authority
LIBOR	London Interbank Offering Rate
LIFO	last in, first out
LIR	land-use intensity rating
Lis/P	lis pendens

LLC	limited liability company
L.P.	land patent
LOC	line of credit
LOI	letter of intent
L/O	lease option
L/P	lease purchase
LP	limited partnership
LPOA	limited power of attorney
LS	landlord seller; locus sigilli (Latin— "place of seal")
LSR	livability space ratio
LTV, L/V	loan-to-value
LUI	land-use intensity
LUL	land use law
LUMS	land utilization marketing study
LUST	leaking underground storage tank

M

MBR	master bedroom
MBS	mortgage-backed security
MACRS	modified accelerated cost recovery system

MF	multifamily
MGRAD	minimum guidelines and requirements for accessible design
MGRM	monthly gross rent multiplier
MIP	mortgage insurance premium
MIS	management information system
MLP	master limited partnership
MLS	multiple-listing service
MPR	minimum property requirement
MRB	mortgage reserve bond
MSA	metropolitan statistical area
MSDSs	material safety data sheets
MUD	municipal utility district

N

n/a	not available or not applicable
NC	not connected (sewer)
NLA	net leasable area
NNN	triple net lease
NOI	net operating income
NOL	net operating loss

NOO	nonowner occupant
NOW	negotiable order of withdrawal
NPL	national priorities list
NRA	net rentable area
NRV	net realizable value
NSF	not sufficient funds

O

OAR	overall rate
OER	operating expense ratio
O/F	owner financing
OE&T	operating expenses and taxes
OIR	official interpretation rulings
OL&T	owners', landlords', and tenants' liability insurance
OO	owner occupant
ORE	owned real estate
OTC	over the counter

P

PAM	pledged account mortgage
PB	principal broker
PC	participation certificate

PCB	polychlorinated biphenyls
PCi/L	picocuries per liter of air
PD-H	planned development housing
PE	professional engineer
P&I	principal and interest
P&L	profit and loss
P&S	purchase and sale agreement
PITI	principal, interest, taxes, and insurance (monthly payments)
PMI	private mortgage insurance
PMM	purchase-money mortgage
POA	power of attorney
POB	point of beginning
POC	paid outside of closing
PRD	planned residential development
PRM	permanent reference marker
PRP	potentially responsible party
PSC	participation sale certificate
PUD	planned unit development

R	
R	REALTOR®
RA	REALTOR® ASSOCIATE®
RAM	reverse annuity mortgage
REA	reciprocal easement agreement
REC	real estate commission
REIT	real estate investment trust
REO	real estate owned
Rm	room
ROI	return on investment
RRM	renegotiable rate mortgage
RS	revenue stamp
RTO	rent to own
RV	recreational vehicle
R/W	right-of-way

S	
S	section
SAM	shared appreciation mortgage
SBLN	setback line
SBS	sick building syndrome

SF	square feet
SFH	single-family house
SFR	single-family residence
S&L	savings and loan association
SMSA	standard metropolitan statistical area
SOYD	sum of the years' digits
SS	scilicet (Latin—"namely")

T

T/B	tenant buyer
T/C	tenant in common
TCT	transfer certificate of title
TDD	telecommunication devices for deaf
TDI	temporary disability insurance
TDR	transfer of development rights
T/E	tenancy by the entirety
TSO	time-share ownership

U

UBIT	unrelated business income tax
UCC	uniform commercial code
UCR	usual, customary, and reasonable

UFFI	urea-formaldehyde foam installation
URAR	Uniform Residential Appraisal Report
USPAP	Uniform Standards of Professional Appraisal Practice
UST	underground storage tank

V–Z

VA	Veterans Administration
VOCs	volatile organic compounds
VRM	variable-rate mortgage
v.	versus
WROS	with right of survivorship
W/W	wall to wall
YTD	year-to-date
Z	zone

CONSTRUCTION DIAGRAMS

1st FLOOR

BASEMENT

ONE-STORY HOUSE

EXPANSION
ATTIC

1st FLOOR

BASEMENT

ONE-AND-A-HALF-STORY HOUSE

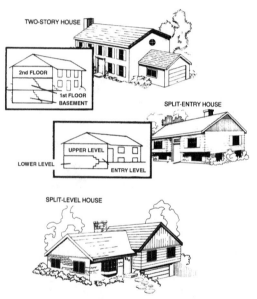

TWO-STORY HOUSE

2nd FLOOR

1st FLOOR

BASEMENT

SPLIT-ENTRY HOUSE

UPPER LEVEL

LOWER LEVEL

ENTRY LEVEL

SPLIT-LEVEL HOUSE

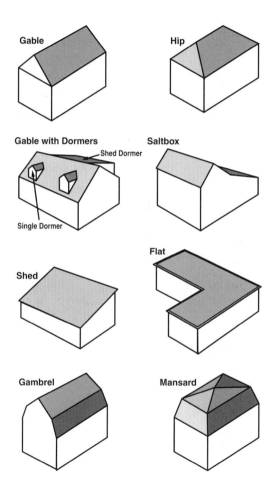

Gable

Hip

Gable with Dormers

Shed Dormer

Single Dormer

Saltbox

Shed

Flat

Gambrel

Mansard

Double-hung

Horizontal Sliding

Casement

Jalousie

Storm

Fixed

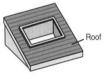
Roof

Skylight

Panel

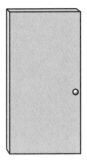

Flush

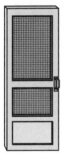

Screen Door

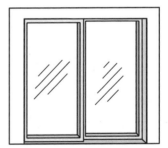

Sliding Glass

About the Author

John W. Reilly, DREI, is a graduate of Hamilton College and Fordham Law School in New York. A former U.S. Army legal officer, he has been a member of the New York, California, Hawaii, and Federal Bars, as well as a REALTOR® and a licensed real estate broker in Hawaii and California. Mr. Reilly practiced real estate law in Honolulu, Hawaii. He previously was an adjunct professor of real estate law and licensed real estate instructor for both salesperson and broker classes. Mr. Reilly has served as Educational Consultant to Hawaii's Real Estate Commission and is the Real Estate Testing Consultant to Applied Measurement Professionals (AMP). He is author of the leading text on agency, *Agency Relationships in Real Estate,* and is co-author of the book *Questions and Answers to Help You Pass the Real Estate Exam.*

He is a past president of the Real Estate Educators Association and the recipient of its Real Estate Educator of the Year Award. He is vice-president of Real Estate Electronic Publishing, an Internet focused company he co-founded in 1995, and the InternetCrusade®, a Web presence provider (see *www.InternetCrusade.com*) and developer of a number of online real estate courses including the National Association of REALTORS® e-PRO Technology Certification Program.

About the Contributing Editor

Marie S. Spodek, DREI, has been teaching sales-person and broker pre-licensing classes and continuing education classes for more than twenty-five years. A popular speaker, trainer, and former real estate columnist, she is the author of *Environmental Issues in Your Real Estate Practice*, a consulting editor for *Property Management, Seventh Edition*, co-author of *Manufactured and Modular Housing* and *Insurance for Consumer Protection: What Every Agent Should Know,* and editorial project consultant for Dearborn's *Real Estate Basics* and *Exam Preps*.

Ms. Spodek has been actively involved with The Real Estate Educator's Association (REEA) since 1987, and in 2001, it awarded her the first Jack Wiedemer Distinguished Career Award. She is a graduate of Augustana College (SD), a former Fulbright Scholar to India, and a frequent world traveler.